ARE YOU WISHING YOUR LIFE AWAY?

From Anxiety to Enthusiasm:
Setting Goals for your Life

By Charles Hughes, MA, LCPC

ISBN: 0615716911

ISBN 13: 9780615716916

Library of Congress Number: 2012919908

First Paperback Publication

Almond inYour Head Books

December, 2012

For my dad, Glen Ellsworth Hughes (1909 — 1990),
who loved to tell me stories.

Acknowledgments

My thanks to my buddy and motivational speaker, Greg Risberg, MSW, CSP, for listening to my idea for this book, encouraging me and suggesting the book's title. For more information about Greg, see www.GregRisberg.com "Humor, With a Message."

My deep gratitude to many other people who blew wind into my sails when I had doubts about changing careers, writing this book, trusting the future. Doubts are the foul winds that blow us off course. Without the support of others, we are lost.

Please visit my webpage:
www.chughes-cms.com
and my blog
www.almondhead.wordpress.com

Please note that any hypothetical examples I have provided in this book are fictional. Any similarities to facts communicated to me by clients are purely coincidental.

Contents

"Who wants to live a life imprisoned by safety?"
From the movie "Amelia," attributed to Amelia Earhart,
first woman to fly solo, non-stop across the Atlantic.

"Winning isn't everything. But wanting to win is."
—Vince Lombardi, coach of the Green Bay Packers,
winner of the first two Super Bowls

"No battle was ever won according to plan, but no battle was ever won without one."
— General Dwight Eisenhower, Supreme Commander of the Allied
Forces in WWII and 34th President of the United States

"I have been absolutely terrified every moment of my life—and I have never let it keep me from doing a single thing I wanted to do."
—Georgia O'keeffe (artist and author)

Introduction

In 1972, at age twenty-two, I became a computer programmer. I loved it. "I get paid to solve puzzles," I used to say. After about fifteen years, I started leading projects, so I changed my job description to, "I get paid to plan problems."

Ten more years zipped by. Good paychecks, good benefits, good grief!—I was bored, and even worse, I was out-distanced by twenty-two year olds who knew the newer technologies (for example, the Internet) better than I did.

I went back to school to update my skills in computer science. To my dismay, I discovered I was bored by the new technologies. Bored and out of date are a bad combination, leading to a loss of self-esteem and other not-so-good things.

I thought about changing careers. What did I do?

I sat on my fanny for another four years until September 11, 2001.

The victims of 911 woke up that day thinking they had their lives to realize their dreams. There is always tomorrow. As I recovered from the shock of our national complacency, I also recovered from mine.

In 2002, I went back to school for a master's degree in Marriage and Family Counseling. I did more than that. I decided I was going to get licensed and open a private practice that would allow me to set my hours, decide my own priorities, and be the captain of my own destiny.

People ask me how I chose counseling after thirty years in corporate information technology. How you choose a new career is a different book. I will say this. I understood that when I was twenty, technology interested me. When I was fifty, people interested me.

The hard part, of my career change, was letting go of my fear of being on my own, with no company providing the illusion of security. The hard part was to decide to rely on myself and commit myself to a goal. That is what I want you to think about, *for your life*, as you read this book.

In my practice, I specialize in helping people with anxiety and its ugly stepsister, depression. They go together. The best anti-anxiety medication in the world is not a GABA Enhancer (like Xanax). My Rx for depression and anxiety is a GOYA (Get off your ass) pill.

> *The hard part was to decide to rely on myself.*

I have compassion for people who have suffered for years from anxiety and depression. I understand that for many of these individuals life seems colorless, tasteless, and full of risks. That is why I chose to work with these clients. I don't claim that anxiety and depression are not real. The experience of anxiety or depression is real.

I want to change the way you think about fear and anxiety. I want you to stop thinking of it as a normal response to life, or as an abnormal problem (disorder) that eventually comes to ruin your life.

I want you to start thinking of anxiety as a way of avoiding life. The technical psychobabble for that is a "defense." A defense is a thought, behavior, or feeling that lets you avoid a more uncomfortable thought, behavior, or feeling.

What is more uncomfortable than anxiety? That is the question you should be asking. What emotion or behavior is so uncomfortable that you would rather be scared or anxious instead? The answer will be unique to you and it may surprise you.

Yet, if you find that answer, you will have the "cure" for your fears, phobias, and anxieties.

This book is a personal odyssey. I was a shy child. I grew up with anxieties and experienced them through a part of my adult life. Plus, I spent much of my life trying to be safe. What I have to offer you is my experience that living with these limitations is not necessary. You can live free of fear and achieve the things you want. I know that because I did it—and I know others who have done it.

If you are determined to believe that you suffer from an anxiety disorder and that the only solution is a constant supply of medication, then I wish you the best. There may be little of value for you in these pages. You may even find some of my statements naïve or unsympathetic. All I can ask is that you read on and keep an open mind.

I don't want you to feel better about life. I want you to get down-home, giddy, grinning, and excited about life. We're going to look at some anxieties and see them for what they are: frauds and phantoms come to scare the child in us.

You can begin now, by asking: How do I want to walk this Earth?

Walking the Earth

My dad died in 1990 at age eighty-one.

At the wake, called a visitation where I come from, I stood in front of his casket and thought, "his time to walk the Earth is over." I began to think about my death and pictured myself, there in that casket, an old man, and I was shaken by the inevitable thought that someday my time to walk the Earth will be over.

How do you want to walk the Earth?

I do not mean to conjure up platitudes about being a good person, or helping others, or being an agent of change, or anything you do outside yourself.

Picture your feet on the Earth, whether it is a sidewalk or gravel road or grassy meadow. You are walking, putting one foot on the ground and then the other. You get to do this for about four score years. After that, you will never again walk down the street and see people going about their business, or the traffic light changing, or the flowers blooming in a meadow.

You will never walk into a coffee shop, smell the fragrance, and stand, with your legs shuffling impatiently as you wait for the clerk to take your order. Never again will you walk into the sunshine and sit with your feet on the Earth while you sip your latte.

Your life of limitless exploration started when you took your first step as a child. Walking this Earth has taken you everywhere you ever went. Even when a car, bus, plane, or boat intervened, you still had to walk on and off that car, bus, plane, or boat.

How often do you feel the weight of your body against the soles of your feet as you walk? How often do you walk until your feet are tired and sit to savor the aches in your legs? Those aches say you are alive.

Your time to walk will be over someday. With a little care and a bit of luck, you will walk to the place where your heart runs out of juice and your legs are too tired to stand one more time.

Then others will walk around the casket where you lie. They will look down on you, and then walk away and talk with others. People will be walking around the room, perhaps talking about you, or perhaps about a new movie. They might remark that you would have liked this movie.

How do you want to walk the Earth?

Do you want to walk it in a hurry or in fear of what is around the next corner?

You started walking as a child for the pure joy of being able to do so. Later you started walking with a purpose, to get somewhere. You sure went to a lot of places, didn't you?

Now, your time to walk is over.

What if, when you are in that casket, a voice whispers in your ear, "I will give you one more hour to walk the Earth? Consider it a bonus. That's one hour. Then you are right back here and that lid will close forever."

Where would you walk? How would you walk? What would you look at? Would you pound your footfalls into the Earth to get every ounce of feeling you could get from it? Would your eyes burn to see each miracle they could see: a tree, a flower, two people holding hands, a dog wagging its tail, a child looking up at you with eyes that still see treasures in the everyday things of life?

How would you spend that hour walking? Would you revel in being alone to explore the same old world you ignored for fifty or sixty years? Would you walk hand-in-hand with that person you left behind, listening for the comforting clatter of her heels against the ground and feel the unbearable delight of the way her arm swings with yours in cadence with your steps?

How would you walk the Earth if you had one more hour?

Please let me figure that out before my time to walk is over.

I hope I would walk boldly, my shoes clocking on the pavement, my shoulders in a confident and friendly swagger. I hope my face would greet the world with a "Hey, it's not that badass of a life" grin. I hope people seeing me walk that way would take a deep breath and feel the air in their lungs and be more grateful because they can still walk the Earth.

I'd say to them, "Stranger, I have to go now. My time to walk this Earth is over. I had a good walk. You have a good walk too."

Part 1: Getting to Know Your Fears

—✺—

The Almond in Your Head

You have decided that you want to walk the Earth without fear. Yet, fear and anxiety have been a common theme in your life. You may or may not qualify for a specific diagnosis, but you find yourself not doing things because of fear, or not enjoying what you do, to the fullest, because you are nervous or anxious.

Computer scientists call your brain a neural network. Your brain is made of about 100,000,000,000 cells, called neurons. To provide some perspective, the estimated number of domain names on the Internet (for example, www.chughes-cms.com) is 142,000,000. Your brain has seven hundred times as many cells as the Internet has places you can visit.

The neurons in your brain are connected in complex ways that science is beginning to explore. The way your brain is connected, at any moment, determines how you respond to the world *at that moment*. (For more on this see "Synaptic Self" in Further Reading.)

The brain does two things well. First, it likes to do the same thing today that it did yesterday. That is called habituation. Second, it likes to learn new things and rewire itself. That is called plasticity.

Habits and learning are what we do. Mostly, we are following habits. What would happen if every morning you had to decide which hand you will use to brush your teeth? *Let's see, yesterday I brushed with my right hand. What are the pros and cons of using my left hand today?* Without habits, we would get little done. Our habits make almost all our decisions for us. That's both good and bad.

If one of the habits we have burned into our neurons is always looking for what can go wrong, we may be reluctant to try new things.

Life has its dangers, and evolution has programmed our brains to pay attention to them. Nature provided us with a threat detector in our heads.

> *Our habits make almost all our decisions for us. That's both good and bad.*

Anatomists named it "the almond" because of its shape. Latin was fashionable at the time, so they used the word: amygdala.

The amygdala makes a quick assessment of a situation and rates it for threat potential. If it perceives a threat, it sends messages directly to several parts of the brain, bypassing the thinking areas (prefrontal cortex). It responds faster than your eyes do in perceiving a threat. The goal is to make you "feel something is wrong" before your conscious mind is aware that something is wrong.

The amygdala is evolution's smoke-detector and it tends to see threats everywhere. Alerting us that there is a stick next to our foot is better than ignoring a snake. For jungles, this was top-notch engineering. The amygdala has its drawbacks in a world of sudden noises, traffic, economic downturns, crime, evil bosses, and media paranoia.

If your general outlook is fearful, your smoke alarm may be going off when the smoke comes from the neighbors roasting weenies on a grill.

How the Almond Works

You're crossing the street. Suddenly, your body tingles, your heart rate increases, you freeze and, from the corner of your eye you detect something. This all happened in a fraction of a second. You look to your right and see a car heading straight for you. Your heart pounds and you dash for the other side of the street. The driver honks his horn and gives you an angry look. You stand there catching your breath and after a few minutes you're calmer.

You've just experienced a fear response, developed through evolution and built into your brain to help you survive. You knew the car was there before you consciously saw it. Or more accurately, your brain knew the car was there. Your brain initiated the actions that may have saved your life.

When the amygdala senses a threat, it sends out messages to many parts of the brain. The messages cause chemicals, such as norepinephrine, to be released into our brains and into our blood. Norepinephrine is one of the chemicals that produces a "fight-or-flight response." The result is to speed up the heart, increasing blood supply to the large skeletal muscles, pump-up glucose in the blood-stream, and send oxygen to the brain. Most important, we become more aware of our surroundings.

For a diagram showing this amygdalar response, see "The Threat Circuit" in the appendices.

Researchers call this an "emotional behavior" and it is common to all animals similar to us, other mammals such as cats and dogs, for example. We do not control this behavior. We do not create it; our brains do it for us. We cannot stop it from happening.

When this emotional response is strong, we become aware of it. We report that we feel something. What we feel differs from person to person but it is usually not comfortable. Our emotional response tells us to pay attention to that car speeding toward us as we cross the street. Brain researcher, Antonio Demasio, has called this "the feeling of what happens."

The fear response makes us aware of the car coming at us and prepares us to take rapid action, which in this case is getting out of the way.

When evolution created our frontal lobes, especially the part called the pre-frontal cortex, we acquired the ability to think about things that are not happening. This ability allows us to anticipate possible future events. It also allows us to imagine threats. When we do, we set off our brain's threat management system.

Our amygdala can't tell a real threat from an imagined threat. The same chemical and physical changes happen in our brain and body that happened when that car was coming at us. No threat exists, but there is nothing to stop the built-in threat response either. We go on being afraid. That's the problem. At this point we usually call the ongoing response "anxiety." Anxiety is fear of something that is not happening.

Yet, our anxieties can feel so darn real.

Can you quiet your amygdala? You can learn mental and behavioral exercises that will help. Most of you have read about or learned these techniques elsewhere. I describe a few of them in the appendices, under "Simple Strategies for Fear and Anxiety" and "The Breath of Life."

> *Anxiety is fear of something that is not happening.*

We're going to focus here on changing your beliefs about fear and anxiety, re-channeling fear and anxiety into hope and enthusiasm. I'm betting that the more hopeful and enthusiastic you become, the more you're going to ignore your fears.

Ignoring Your Fears (How to be a happy fool)

Did I say, ignore your fears?

Sounds foolish, right?

Yet, that's our goal. I am going to give you a simple process for doing it. You can stop reading and practice for a few days. After that, you may be saying that Charles Hughes LCPC is an idiot. His advice does not work and I wasted my money on this book.

Please come back and read more.

Step 1: Recognize the Fear

Problem Belief: If I don't admit I am afraid, I won't feel afraid.

This may sound unnecessary. I've found that many people don't stop and notice they're feeling fearful, or they don't want to admit it. You must do this. Say it aloud. "I am feeling fearful or anxious." When you deny a feeling, you short circuit your brain's way of telling you to pay attention to something.

Step 2: Take Responsibility for the Fear

Problem Belief: The cause of my fear is outside me

What to do:

Identify the fear. Ask what it is you're feeling fearful or anxious about. Here is the question you must ask and you must ask it exactly this way: "What am I scaring myself about?" By asking the question this way, you are taking responsibility for your fears. Phrase your answer as "I am scaring myself that fill-in-the-blank is going to happen."

The cause of your fear is inside you.

Step 3: Name the Fear

Problem Belief: All my fears are real

What to do:

You must stop believing that all your fears are real. Most of them are not. But how do you know? I have done more than sixty-two years of extensive research and identified four fear types: Ostriches, Bogeymen, Heebie-Jeebies, and Webejamins. Ask what kind of fear this is?

Fear type 1: Ostriches

An Ostrich is a fear of an event that you can change or stop. The problem is that you have your head in the sand like an Ostrich.

Example of this type of fear: I'm scaring myself that I will fail my math test tomorrow. Solution: Put down your iphone or the TV remote and study.

Fear type 2: Bogeymen

A Bogeyman is fear about something unlikely to occur. Many of your fears are Bogeymen. As kids, we were always waiting for that Bogeyman to jump out of the closet. How do you handle a Bogeyman? Calm yourself; distract yourself.

Make fun of this kind of fear. Give the Bogeyman a name, Freddie maybe, and say "Hey, Freddie, come out of that closet and have a soda with me. What's the skinny on being a Bogeyman, anyway?"

You may find that this is hard. Many of us have tuned our brains to see Bogeymen everywhere. This is when "Step 4 — Ignore the Fear" (see below) must become a new habit. In Step 4, I offer you a "Mantra for Ignoring My Fears."

Use this mantra or, better yet, make up your own mantra. Make using it a new habit. At first, this will seem artificial and unhelpful. Keep doing it. With practice, it will become second nature.

Example of this type of fear: What if I lose my job? Is there any evidence that you are going to lose your job? If not, this is a Bogeyman. If there is evidence such as rumors of downsizing, this fear becomes an Ostrich. Check out the rumors. Is there any substance to them? If not, take a breath and use your mantra. If there is, polish your resume and start job hunting.

Fear type 3: Heebie-jeebies

A Heebie-Jeebie is something unpleasant that you *want to happen* and you are scaring yourself that it may go wrong.

Distract and calm yourself. Forget about it! Meditate (pray), listen to music, engage in an activity you enjoy. Breathe, breathe, breathe. See "The Breath of Life" in appendices for more on calming practices.

Example of this type of fear: I have a surgery tomorrow and I am scaring myself that something bad will happen.

Fear type 4: Webejamins

Webejamins are my favorite type of fear. A Webejamin is something *good* that you *want* to happen and you are scaring yourself that something may go wrong. What you are avoiding is excitement. I find these Webejamins are what I get the most anxious about. I bypass excitement, go right into anxiety, dive under the covers and turn the electric blanket up to nine.

The antidote for this fear is to get excited about it. Think wonderful thoughts. Call your friends and tell them about it. Tell your amygdala to go to hell.

Example: you have a job interview tomorrow and you are scaring yourself that you will screw it up. Get excited about it. Your fear is nothing more than a smokescreen keeping you from feeling hope and enthusiasm.

A job interview might also be an Ostrich because you may be worrying about the interview instead of preparing for it. Get online, find out about the company. Practice answering questions they might ask. Accept a little nervousness as stage fright. Most performers say stage fright is important because it tunes you up and gives you an edge.

Step 4: Ignore the Fear

Problem Belief: If I stop thinking about it, something bad will happen

What to do:

You have identified your fear as an Ostrich, Bogeyman, Heebie-Jeebie or Webejamin. You have decided to take the proper corrective action:

Stop being scared about not being scared.

fix the problem (study), calm yourself, distract yourself, or get excited. Now, you are worried about not being worried.

Mantra for Ignoring My Fears

I promised you a mantra for ignoring your fears. Here it is. Use this or make up your own. Use it everyday. In time, it will be like carrying around a good luck charm. Your brain will learn to react to it by calming down. It will take time and persistence. Start using it today.

My fears are an overactive amygdala. My fears mean nothing. I will feel hopeful and enthusiastic rather than fearful and pessimistic. I will not be afraid. I will not even think about being afraid. I would rather be a happy-go-lucky fool than walk this Earth as a scaredy cat.

Spend a few days trying these four steps and your mantra for managing fear and anxiety. Be a happy fool for a week. See how it feels. See what you learn about yourself. Keep a notebook about how you scare yourself. If you need more help, come back.

You're Back

What would it be like never to be afraid again? "Impossible," you say. "We all have fears," you say. You would be right about that. Nearly everyone has something they scare themselves about. Some people are able to shrug off anything while others state that they are not able to not worry.

Do you think you were born worrying?

You may have been told that anxiety is genetic; it runs in families. Many things run in families, including most of our likes and dislikes. Is liking your mother's goulash genetic? You learned to like your mother's goulash either because your mother's goulash is top notch or because you wanted her to feel appreciated.

I sincerely doubt they will ever find an anxiety gene. We may find some genes that make someone vulnerable to anxiety, but vulnerable is not helpless. They haven't found those genes yet. For the sake of what follows, can we agree that, at least in part, your anxieties and fears are something you learned? If you learned them, you can unlearn them.

Consider the places you might be stuck. They fall into three categories related to three of the problem beliefs stated in the section above:

- *Stuck Point 1: The cause of my fear is outside me*
- *Stuck Point 2: All my fears are real*
- *Stuck Point 3: If I stop thinking about it something bad will happen.*

Stuck Point 1: The Cause of My Fear is Outside Me

Running from the Bear

"Do we run from a bear because we are afraid, or are we afraid because we run?" (William James as paraphrased by Joseph LeDoux)

I find that my natural way of thinking is that I act a certain way because I feel something. For example, I feel anxious or fearful, so I want to avoid the thing I think is making me feel that way. I want to look outside myself for the sources of my fears.

In 1884, psychologist William James suggested something which has been supported by brain scientists today. He suggested that our emotions are reactions to how we react to an event, not to the event itself.

William James' Revolutionary Idea:
William James suggested that our emotions result from how we perceive and react to an event, not to the event itself.

He used a famous example: Do we run from a bear because we are afraid, or are we afraid because we run from the bear? He reasoned that our fear is the result of how we behave, including our physiological changes, in response to the bear. You can read more about this in Chapter 3 of *The Emotional Brain* by Joseph LeDoux.

When I tell people about William James' bear, they usually say, "Yeah, so you don't run from the bear and he eats you. Tell me about that Mr. Know-It-All therapist." William James' bear is a symbol of our fears. What the person is asking is "What if I don't run (act on my fears) and I get run over by life?"

That reminds me of a story.

Two guys are going on a nature walk. One shows up wearing running shoes. His friend asks him what the running shoes are for.

"Just in case we run into any bears," he replies.

His friend scoffs and asks, "You think those shoes will let you outrun a bear."

"No," the other guy says, "but I don't need to outrun the bear. I just need to outrun you."

Here is the bad news. Life is going to run over you sometimes. Some of life's bears jump out from behind trees and you have no time to run; sometimes you can't outrun bears that are faster than you.

Here is the good news. I think *getting run over by life is better than sitting on the sidelines.* That is my opinion and you can disagree.

A reporter in Chicago interviewed a young African American girl for a news story and asked her why bad things happen to people.

She shrugged and said, "Well, sometimes you eat the bear and sometimes the bear eats you."

Wisdom from a child and I bet she never read William James.

Yeah, but you don't have to walk right up to the bear and put your hand in his mouth, is what you are thinking.

> **"Sometimes you eat the bear and sometimes the bear eats you."**

Of course, it's your choice. You can try to outrun life's bears or you can stay fearful and anxious avoiding situations that cause anxiety. Then you're safe, right? If you're so safe, then why are you so fearful and anxious?

Now Hear This — Now Hear This
Every anxiety is a way of grasping or avoiding something.

A Bit of Buddhism

I was packed and ready to load the car, pick up a friend, and head to my favorite water park. I approached my parking space and it was empty. My brain did one of those wonky things as if the car were there; I somehow was not seeing it.

For the briefest moment, I considered that it has been stolen. Then I remembered. *Oh, my gosh, I drove it to the office yesterday, but then I walked home.* My office is about ten minutes away and I normally walk unless the weather is bad. Yesterday, I got in the car and drove. At lunchtime, I walked to the post office, ate lunch, did some errands nearby, and went home.

On foot.

My stomach settled back into a normal state of water park excitement. I picked up my clothing bag and munchies cooler and headed to my office.

You know what happened next

A Bogeymen popped up from behind a mail box and grinned. "What if someone stole you car," he whispered. "Or, more likely, the police towed it from the parking lot. You're going to spend the morning finding where your car is and bailing it out. Your day will be ruined."

One of my anxiety triggers is not knowing what is happening. I can turn a minor unexpected event into an extinction level event. When I do that, I want to know the outcome as fast as possible. I needed to get to my office fast so I walked faster and started breathing more rapidly. My heart sped up. Adrenalin pumped through my body. Those are all symptoms of a panic attack. I do not have panic attacks. I have catastrophic imagination attacks.

I desperately wanted that moment when I would see my car sitting there and know everything was okay.

STOP! JUST STOP!

I talked to myself, saying the following: *You car is sitting in the parking lot at your office and the worst possible thing is that it will have a ticket on it. That is $50.00, not pretty, but not a major problem. I am going to walk more and more slowly and calm myself before I get to my car. I am going to tolerate my uncertainty. Breathe, everything is fine.*

By the time I arrived at my car (not towed away, no ticket), I was calm and feeling good that I had not kept imagining the worst possible outcome. I had been mindful and stayed in the moment.

You can read more about the "Just Stop" technique I used in the appendices at the back of the book. Mindfulness or "staying in the moment" is a Buddhist idea.

Grasping and Avoiding

According to Buddhism, when we encounter something, an object, a person, an event, an idea, we have one of three responses: grasping, avoiding, or ignoring.

When we ignore an idea, experience, or piece of information, we put it away so we do not have to think about it. We may deny that we encountered it. Ignoring is how we protect our viewpoint from inconvenient information.

When we grasp, we want to keep or get more of the thing because it makes us feel good. When we avoid we are trying to keep it from us because it makes us feel bad.

All three reactions are defenses. Both grasping and avoiding can result in anxiety, and the anxiety covers our grasping or avoiding behavior.

When you have a fear or anxiety, ask yourself what you're grasping or avoiding. Maybe you are avoiding looking for a new job (fear of change) or grasping at your current job (sense of security). There are so many situations in which we grasp at one thing or avoid another.

You get a job offer and are feeling anxious rather than excited about the opportunity (an obvious Webejamin) "Why would I avoid excitement?" you ask. We'll get to that later. (See "It's Lonely at the Top.")

You had a date and enjoyed it. Later, you plague yourself with second-guessing every minute of the date. Did your date have fun? Did he/she like you? Will she/he go out with you again? You grasp at the "date experience" because it made you feel good. You want to go on feeling good. That, however, could cause disappointment, if he/she doesn't want to go out with you again.

You want to feel good, so you make yourself miserable. Arrrrrrrrrgh!

Your anxiety over how the date went is either grasping at your desire to go on feeling good or avoiding the possibility that things won't work out. You want to feel good, so you make yourself miserable.

It gets even worse. You make yourself so anxious that you don't call your date for a week. There he/she sits, thinking, *I thought it went so well.* Finally, you call, and guess what, that person you went out with is a bit cool. You think, *she/he really didn't have a good time and doesn't want to go out with me again.* By delaying your call, you turned his/her positive experience into a negative one. We are often the author of our own misery.

If William James was correct, and both Buddhism and neuroscience seems to be saying he was, then it's not the bear that is scaring us, it is our

We are often the author of our own misery.

reaction to the bear that is causing our fear. Our response to the bear is inside us. Grasping and avoiding are inside us.

We're afraid to act, not because of something outside ourselves, but because we don't act. Like a deer staring at an oncoming car, we freeze and then life runs us over and we tell ourselves, "See, I was right not to act." We self-justify our fears and make them real.

When my stepson was ten, I took him to see a movie called "Major League." In this movie, Charlie Sheen plays a baseball pitcher. After the movie, I asked my stepson what he thought. He said that he didn't know Charley Sheen could pitch. Kids sometimes get reality and fantasy mixed up.

That brings us to Stuck Point 2, "All my fears are real."

Remember the monster in your closet when you were a child?

Stuck Point 2: All My Fears Are Real

The Monster in Your Closet

A creaky sound comes from the closet door. You wake feeling uneasy or maybe downright scared. Your little hands pull the covers up and you squint through the darkness at the closet door. *There is nothing there*, you tell yourself silently but your six-year old mind cannot make you believe it. You know there are monsters. You have seen them on the TV and in storybooks. You want to be brave and on most nights you succeed, but not tonight. Tonight, you begin to cry as quietly as you can. You are sure the door opened a bit. Not much, though, and only you would notice it. The monster is too much for you and you cry for mom or dad. They chase the monster away, for tonight at least.

Then you grow up and you make a deal with the monster. You agree you're no longer afraid of such things. You're grown up now. You feel better and for years the monster seems to have disappeared.

Only it hides in your dreams and you wake in the middle of the night. You are in a cold sweat. You smile uneasily because last night your four-year-old son called you in to his room to deal with his monster. Unlike your yellow-eyed closet monster, his is a snaky thing that lives under his bed. You're so glad you are a grown-up now. You know that there are no monsters under beds or in the closet.

And your monster waits patiently.

Until one day, your life hits a big snag. Maybe it's a divorce or a lost job, or a death in the family or an illness, anything that knocks your carefully constructed adult mind off balance. One night you wake shaking and look at the closet. Old Yellow Eyes has been patiently waiting until you are most vulnerable, until things are not going so well and your illusion of safety in life is shattered.

The monster sticks its head out, grins at you and says, "Hello, did you think you could keep me in the closet? Let's do lunch, you and me, like old friends, and talk about what really scares you: what is behind your worst fears. I know you better than anyone. Isn't it time you know me?"

After all these years, with no mommy or daddy to call for help, the monster in the closet slinks out, its eyes glowing, its claws sharp. It pulls down the covers and crawls into bed with you and there is no hope of putting it back in the closet.

Facing Your Real Fears

The monster in your closet was never real. Your parents knew that and if you're now a parent, you know that. What keeps that monster around? It may surprise you, but that monster is there to protect you; to let you avoid something even scarier than a monster. As a child, the monster may have protected you from feeling alone. It gave you an excuse to wake your parents. After all, you can't wake your Dad at 2:00 AM and say, "Gee, Dad, I'm lonely."

Our monsters are there to protect us.

Many things in life have potential for invoking fear: a serious illness, a medical procedure, loss of a job, getting divorced, a math test. The list is endless. I'm going to make a bold statement: none of these things cause us to be afraid. We say, "I'm scared because I have a math test tomorrow." The math test is the trigger for your fear, like William James' bear. The reason for your fear is inside you. The truth is, "I'm scaring myself about the math test tomorrow."

Why are you scaring yourself? What do you need to do? Do you need to prepare more? Are you telling yourself that if you don't do well on this test, something terrible will happen? If what you're scaring yourself about is something you can do something about, then do it.

The math test (monster) is not the source of your fear. What you are avoiding is the source of your fear. Perhaps the problem is that you have been slacking off on the math homework. Here it is the night before the test and you can't make up for weeks of not studying in one night. You may need to change your study habits in the future. Changing your approach to studying may be worse than fear of failing a test. It means self-discipline and sacrificing some face time with your video games or talk time with your friends.

In this case, what you may be avoiding is the truth that you have been slacking off and it's too late to fix it for this test. Change your thinking about this test. How do you change your thinking? *Say to yourself, "I am not prepared for this test and there isn't enough time now to prepare. I may not do very well and I will just have to live with that."*

Maybe you're avoiding something else, like the fact that you don't have any intention of changing your math study habits. If this is the case, you shouldn't expect to do well in math. You will have to accept the consequences of that. What is there to be afraid or anxious about? *You are making a choice not do well in math*

Some would call this mindfulness or staying with yourself in the present. You are accepting the results of your choices. What about the monster in the closet when you were a kid? What would mindfulness look like? *"I am lying here feeling alone and it is unpleasant. I want to avoid it by calling my mom or dad and have them comfort me for a while."* We don't expect that much self-awareness of a child. We allow children their monsters. We don't say, "Stop being a child—there are no monsters." We comfort the child. Later, we can have a talk about monsters.

Being more mindful and self-aware isn't too much to ask of an adult.

One of the fears I often hear from adults today is that they could lose their job. I ask them if they have a current resume and when they last sent out a resume or posted for a job online. They usually give me several reasons that they haven't looked for a better job.

I empathize with them. We've all been there. When people tell me they fear losing their job, what they aren't saying is how unhappy they are with their job. We find it safer to be scared of losing the job we have than to do the tough, sometimes boring work of looking for a another job. Fear of job loss is a common Ostrich fear in a bad economy.

The best way to handle uncertainty is to have options. When that anxious person tells me he sent out some resumes and has an interview next week, he doesn't seem so anxious. Job loss or unemployment is a common trigger for depression and anxiety. See "Setting Goals When You're Unemployed" in the appendices.

If you're nervous about your employment status, and you're doing nothing about it, that is a choice. If you're making a choice, what is there to be anxious about?

When you agree you're making a choice, you no longer need the monster in the closet. Your fear or anxiety is nothing more than a camouflage, a specter, a lie, a sideshow. You're afraid because you're running from what you have to do for a better grade in math, a better relationship, a better job, a better life. We're afraid because we run from the bear. GET IT?

What Are We So Worried About?

"Okay," you say, "I got it. There is no reason to be anxious about the math test or the job. I'll figure out what actions I need to take. But darn it, I still feel anxious. Even when I don't worry, I worry."

Isn't that a bear?

We scare ourselves about not being scared. That brings us to the third stuck point.

Stuck Point 3: If I Stop Worrying, Bad Things Will Happen.

Warding Off, Believing in Magic

You have recognized your fear, taken responsibility for it. You have even named it. You have decided that you can change what you are scaring yourself about (an Ostrich), or concluded that there is nothing you can or want to do about it (a Bogeyman or Heebie-Jeebie). Or it is something you ought be excited about (a Webejamin). *You still don't stop worrying or being anxious.*

Perhaps your logic goes, *if I worry about it, maybe I can avoid the consequences of doing poorly on the math test. Maybe my parents will see how terrible I feel, how worried I am, and not suspend my video game time. Maybe if my boss sees how worried I am about getting the report done by week-end, he won't be upset if I miss his deadline.*

This is called "warding off behavior" and it is the source of most worrying. A "ward" is the outermost part of a castle or fortification. It is also a magic spell used to keep something from happening. (See Appendix: Believing In Magic) A ward also refers to an area of a hospital, where people are sent when they worry too much.

The psychological idea of warding is this. If I think about something enough, it won't happen. If I worry that my boss will give me a bad review, then he won't. Unless, of course, I worry so much I do my job poorly.

How do you not think so much about something going wrong? Sometimes this obsessive thinking is also called "rumination." The *American Heritage College Dictionary* tells us the definition of "to ruminate" is "to turn a matter over and over in the mind."

According to the *Diagnostic and Statistical Manual* published by the American Psychiatric Association, Rumination Disorder is "repeated regurgitating and rechewing of food [after feeding]." Rumination Disorder appears mostly in infants and young children.

Rumination is also the act of an animal, like a cow, chewing on a cud. One approach to worrying less is to make fun of your worries. (see "Really Simple Strategy number 3" in the appendices). You could imagine yourself as a cow, chewing on its cud. The cow is grazing in a field of "Worry Wort," a cousin of St. John's Wort. You could mimic the cow, "moo." I doubt you could think about that and worry at the same time. This gives new meaning to the phrase "Chewing on a problem."

The problem with thinking too much, whether you call it worrying, warding off, or rumination is that it is a self-fulfilling prophecy.

> *One approach to worrying less is to make fun of your worries.*

Most things we worry about don't happen. Our brain keeps getting the message: "See, I worried and it didn't happen; what would have happened if I hadn't worried so much?" Our brain then habituates worrying.

Another justification for worrying that I hear is, "what if something does go wrong and I didn't worry about it and didn't prepare. I would feel like an idiot." When people say this they are confusing worrying with preparing. Remember Ostriches? If there is something you can do about the possible problem, do it. Otherwise, don't pretend you are preparing, just because you are worrying.

"What if something goes wrong," you rejoin.

Something will go wrong and there is nothing much you can do about it. If you worry about ninety-nine things that might go wrong, some of them will go wrong anyway and the one thing you did not worry about or plan for will go wrong too. Life is uncertain. Learn to love it. I don't want you to not be anxious or fearful, I want you to not be anxious or fearful about not being anxious or fearful.

> *I don't want you to not be anxious or fearful, I want you to not be anxious or fearful about not being anxious or fearful.*

I want you to believe, right down in your toes, that you don't have to worry about anything. That you can be a happy fool 97.3% of the time. See Appendix: "Living With Uncertainty."

It's Lonely at the Top

If you remember nothing else, remember this. The scariest words in life are:

- *Success*
- *Joy*
- *Happiness*
- *Peace*
- *Fulfillment*
- *Contentment*
- *Excitement*

How many people do you know who are grooving on life? When we see them, we think they are on drugs. We make up stories about how their lives haven't been as hard as ours or they have something we lack: money, good looks, a great childhood.

If nothing else works to explain their apparent lack of misery, we tell ourselves, they got all the breaks, they are just lucky. Someday, their luck will run out; then they will discover how life is for the rest of us.

One day, something does go wrong for these people. They lose a job in a bad economy. They have a fire in their house. We express our sincerest condolences. Yet, don't we feel just a little relief at their misfortune?

To our astonishment, they groove on. They don't have the sense to know when to be miserable, frightened, and unhappy. *What the hell is wrong with them?*

Misery loves company; misery does not love happiness. When you are happy, some others may resent you. If you are living your life to the fullest, fewer and fewer people are going to understand you, or possibly want to be around you. It's not because people are mean or really want others to suffer. You remind them of what they are not doing in their lives that they so much want to do.

That is what I mean when I say, "It's lonely at the top."

It's risky up there too. The greater your joy, the greater the pain when something goes wrong. To experience great happiness, you will also need to be willing to experience great disappointment, without feeling sorry for yourself, without blaming anyone, without losing faith in yourself or hope for the future.

I want you to try an experiment. Next time you're feeling anxious about something, ask yourself if you could not as easily be excited about it. Sit for a moment, imagining being excited. Then go back to feeling anxious. What you may discover is that the feelings and sensations of anxiety are nearly identical to those of excitement.

> *To experience great happiness, you will also need to be willing to experience great disappointment, without feeling sorry for yourself, without blaming anyone, without losing faith in yourself or hope for the future.*

If you practice, you can go back and forth between excitement and anxiety at will. The word "anxious" has two opposite meaning. He was anxious (worried) about his doctor visit and the children were anxious (excited) for Christmas to come.

It's up to you. Do you want to be worried or excited about life?

How do you want to walk the Earth? If you want to walk with confidence and a happy outlook, you can do it. You may have to give up a few things like worrying, avoiding, grasping. The reward is huge because what you are about to move on to is setting goals. You will ask what you are not doing that you want to do. Doing this from a worried, "what might go wrong," attitude, won't work. From this point on, you need to move forward with excitement, hope, and enthusiasm.

> *You need to move forward with excitement, hope, and enthusiasm.*

Part 2: Setting Goals and Getting on With Life.

—w—

You Can Do Just Fine Without Goals

I went to undergraduate school but never selected a career. I left college with a bachelor's degree but never asked myself what I wanted to do. I went to graduate school at age twenty-three, but I had no plan. I left graduate school because I ran out of money and never returned to that degree program.

Later I went to law school but did not commit myself to finishing that program either. When I was offered a job teaching computer programming, I quit law school. I had no plan, no goal.

I fell into the computer programming mostly by accident because computer jobs were plentiful in the 1970s. Did I like it? It was fine. You can do fine without a plan or a goal. I made a good income and that is what I cared about back then. If you had asked me, I would have told you I was doing just fine.

"Just fine" does not describe a rewarding life. When you are done walking this Earth, do you want to look back and say, "I did just fine?" "Just fine" is safe and doesn't involve taking risks. I spent most of my early life avoiding risk. I was just fine.

While we're talking about "just fine," we may as well discuss its twin sister, "better than I expected." Many people tell you they are doing better than they expected. They may be making a good income, have a great house, money in the bank. Something is missing.

I submit that what is missing is the satisfaction, no, the downright exultation of doing what you want to do. I further submit that what is missing is taking the risk of doing what you want to do. Risk taking is life giving.

Risk taking is life giving.

Imagine two babies, Todd and Bernice, sitting on the floor having the following dialogue:

Todd: Hey, Bernice, what's this thing grown-ups do when they extend their lower appendages, first one, then the other. This appears to propel them across the room.

Bernice: It's called walking, doo-doo brain.

Todd: Looks dangerous to me.

Bernice: I'm sayin'! My mom tries to get me to do it. Puts me up on my feet. Moves me like I'm a little puppet.

Todd: You ought to call child protective services.

Bernice: I can't reach the telephone.

Good thing babies do not worry or scare themselves about taking risks. We would still be walking on all fours and I'd be asking you, "How do you want to crawl the Earth?" We take risks by setting goals, by saying, "Bernice, look at that cool thing grown-ups do. I want to do that."

It's About What You Want to Do

It is not about what you can do. It's about what you want to do. Goals must fire you up. They must make you want to wake up in the morning and put on the coffee.

If you have gotten this far in this book, I hope you have made some progress in turning your fears into enthusiasm and hope. Hope for what? That is where goals come in. If you are actively, every day, nearly every minute, moving toward what you want, you have little time to worry or fret about the future. You are building your future with your two hands. In the process, you're giving meaning to your present.

> *Goals must make you want to wake up and put on the coffee.*

But I don't know what I want?

Believe me, you know what you want. Maybe you don't want to let yourself in on it. Your first goal is to define your goals. No editing, no nay saying, no self-criticism. Remember, it's not about what you can do. It is about what you want to do.

You don't have to know how you are going to do it, just that you want to do it. Can you have anything you want? That is a conundrum. It depends on what you are willing to do. Unfortunately, it also depends on some things you cannot control. Let me offer an example, which, admittedly, will sound crazy.

You would like to have a date with Angelina Jolie or Antonio Banderas if you prefer. "Dream on," you say. "Not possible," you say. Depends on what you are willing to do. That is the first rule of project management: "Is the juice worth the squeeze." We'll get to that in a few pages.

For now, we'll assume you have decided that dating Angie is the most important thing in your life. You are willing to do anything to make it happen. First, what's your time frame? How long do you expect this goal to take? Let's say you decide one year. That makes it long term goal. Any goal that takes a month or more is a long term goal, meaning you have to break it down into pieces. Here is how I break down the goal of dating Angie:

- *Find out where she hangs out.*
- *Find out if she is still with Brad, if so,*
- *Is she happy with Brad?*
- *Arrange to spend time where she hangs out.*
- *Arrange to meet her.*
- *Get to be friends with her.*
- *Ask her out.*

I know you're thinking this is ridiculous and you could never carry out such a plan. Let me translate that negative mindset into a problem-solving mindset. In project management, we never say anything is impossible. We say, *"What are the costs of making it happen?"* If the costs are too high for the benefit derived from the goal, then reevaluate the goal.

You are committed to dating Angie. We will return to commitment many times. Commitment is how you get around roadblocks. Several things can go wrong with the plan. Our mindset is: nothing is a show-stopper; nothing is a problem. All obstacles are challenges to be maneuvered around.

Possible Challenge:
Angie is still hanging out with Brad but rumors are she's not all that happy
Solution: If you are willing to get involved with an attached woman, go forward.

Possible Challenge: Angie is still with Brad and rumor is that she is really happy.
Solution: This may require re-evaluating the goal. I hear Brad can throw a mean punch. If you want to go forward, consider Karate lessons.

Possible Challenge: Angie is very hard to meet and is usually with a three-hundred pound bodyguard.

Solution: Meet some of her friends first, to gain her trust.

Investigate bribing the bodyguard. Take more Karate lessons.

Possible Challenge: You met her but she just wants to be friends, not go out with you.

Solution: No different from any other possible dating situation; how far are you willing to go to change her mind?

Possible Challenge: She says yes, she'll go out with you but only if you take her to Honolulu on your date (Hey, she's a high-maintenance woman.)

Solution: If you want to go out with her, pony up.

Slightly Sneaky Solution: Ask her to have a coffee with you to discuss plans for the trip.

Obviously, if you are willing to go to that length to date Angelina Jolie, your goal should probably be "Get over your obsession with Angie." Then the steps would be things like: find a good psychotherapist.

My scenario has two points. First, is this goal something you really want, or a nice fantasy, not a goal? The measure of this is whether the goal is worth the cost. The first rule of project management says: *Is the juice worth the squeeze?*

The second point is that lots of things can go wrong with any project plan. You have to constantly re-plan to get to the goal. The second principle of project management says: *Things change. Nothing ever works the way you planned it.*

The Five Steps to Achieving Goals

I spent thirty years in the corporate world, working on and managing projects. Over the years, the words used in project management changed many times. The basic process never changed. Based on the principles of project management, there are five steps to achieving a goal:

- *Acknowledge the goal as yours*
- *Actualize the goal by stating it to yourself and publicly*
- *Activate resources: planning with The Four Rules of Project Management*
- *Act by taking the necessary steps*
- *Achieve by behaving as if you have reached the goal*

The order of these steps is important. They go from "more abstract" to "more concrete." Early steps toward a goal are usually not very costly. Later steps can involve concrete actions such as taking out a bank loan, or moving to another part of the country. The most important cost of a project is your time. You only have so much of it. You want to commit your time to the most important goals.

Building your commitment and your plan gives you time to think and adds confidence to your decision to achieve this goal. Planning allows time to modify the goal if need be.

Actuating the goal, which includes telling other people has a dual purpose. First, it allows other people to provide input to your plan. This is especially important with people who have done what you intend to do. You will also run into nay-sayers who may tell you why you can't do what you want to do. Some people told me that I was crazy to change careers so close to retirement. Many more people told me how envious they were that I was doing so.

The second advantage in telling others about your goal is accountability. Telling other people may seem risky. You may ask, "what if I fail to achieve the goal? That would be embarrassing.

There is No Such Thing as Failure.

Often people say we don't set goals because we are afraid of failing. In my opinion, the concept of "failure" is nothing but a way of characterizing an outcome.

We take an action or we don't act; either way there will be an outcome. That outcome will have consequences, good, bad, or both. When we accept an outcome that is not what we wanted, we make a decision. Let's use an example.

You want to learn to play a musical instrument, perhaps the guitar. You buy a guitar and start taking lessons. You do well at first; then it gets harder. You decide not to practice as much because it is not as much fun. Of course, we don't call that a decision; we just don't practice as much. When you attend your lessons, it is uncomfortable because you don't play as well as you expected. Maybe the teacher has to correct you more often. You get discouraged, which is just another decision. After a while, you stop practicing altogether, which is another decision. It shows in your lessons. You tell yourself *this isn't fun anymore. Maybe the guitar isn't my thing.* That is another decision. Then you quit lessons.

Did you fail to learn the guitar? Not at all. You succeeded in learning something about playing the guitar. You did not stick with it long enough to play well. You decided not to learn to play better.

I think "failure" was invented by schools. Where did you first hear the word "fail?" We are told we "failed" a test. The truth is that we achieved a score on the test that teachers call a failing score. What if they called it a "low score" instead? That would be descriptive without adding the judgment implied by the word failure.

We learned about failure in school and then carried that lesson into adulthood. I submit that there is no such thing as failure. There are only an outcome and the consequences of that outcome. Sometimes we say we failed when all we did was make a decision.

Go back to Angie.

Suppose after you met Angie, she refused to go out with you. You come back from your mission saying, "I failed." The reality is that you have chosen not to pursue the goal anymore. This may be a totally rational decision. So often, people decide to give up on a goal because they hit a roadblock. They decide that getting around this roadblock is not worth the effort. This is not failure; it is a decision.

I am concerned with this idea of failure when it comes to children, especially teens. Teenagers have enough to deal with today. They don't need this judgment of failure, either from parents or teachers. By the time kids are teens, they are so indoctrinated about failure that I often cannot get them to rethink the idea. When I tell them that there is no such thing as failure, there is only an outcome, they say, "Tell that to my parents and teachers."

> *There is no such thing as failure.*

Why We Don't Set Goals

I think we don't set goals because we are afraid to succeed. Success is lonely. There it is. The more you set and achieve goals, the more you may be the object of envy, criticism, and misunderstanding. Your detractors will say you don't deserve what you have or you were lucky or you don't have problems as tough or serious as theirs.

Some of your friends will say, "Oh, I am so happy for you," and all the while, smile a bit every time you have a setback. *That doesn't mean they're not your friends.* It means they are human and they have some goals and needs they aren't working on.

You may have learned in childhood that to out-achieve your friends, or your parents, was risky. You might not be liked as much. You decided it was better to be liked than lonely. Get used to it. Success can be lonely sometimes.

> *"Happiness is a state of activity." — Aristotle.*

Why bother setting goals? The process of acknowledging your goals and acting on them gets us out of being anxious or depressed or unhappy. Happiness is not a state of being. As the Greek philosopher, Aristotle, said, "Happiness is a state of activity."

Achieve – Gesundheit!

When I opened my counseling practice, I had an office, a telephone, some furniture. I had a website. Decorating the office was fun. I had total freedom to do whatever I wanted.

My practice was small. That's all I thought about. I did not feel successful. I didn't use the word "practice" when I talked to friends. When they asked me how it was going, I said "Okay, kind of slow."

I had reached my goal, but I was not acting like it. It was months before I said to people, "I have a private practice. My office is in downtown Oak Park."

"Achieving" is acting as if you have reached a goal. It is the payoff, the prize, the champagne. It's the fuel that motivates you to set a new goal.

When you have reached a goal, you need to act like it. Brag about it.

> *Achieving is acting as if you have reached a goal. It is the payoff, the prize, the champagne.*

Advertise it. Celebrate it. Make your friends jealous. Maybe then they will start working on some of their dormant goals. Then you can celebrate with them and it won't be so lonely at the top.

Let's Talk More About Happiness.

"I just want to be happy."

Have you ever said that to yourself or someone else? If not, I will bet someone has said it to you. If there is anything that we spend a lot of time chasing, it is happiness. The experts call it "subjective well-being." What are some of the commonly heard ideas about happiness?

- *We all know you can't buy it.*
- *If you chase happiness it runs from you.*
- *Happiness is a state of mind.*
- *Happiness is a decision you make.*

The first belief reminds me of the words of actress Bo Derrick, whom you may remember from the movie "10." She said, "Whoever said you can't buy happiness didn't know where to go shopping."

Of course, you can buy happiness. Things I have bought that made me happy are:

- *A new car*
- *An ice-cream cone*
- *A Hawaiian Vacation*
- *My Kindle Ereader*
- *My new stove*

You are probably saying, "Yeah, but those things only make you happy for a while." You would be right about that. Nothing makes you happy forever. People who rely on buying things to make them happy are chasing happiness.

What about that chasing happiness thing?

When I was a teenager, I knew a strange man. His eyes were always crossed, giving him a disturbing and penetrating gaze.

One day he turned that gaze on me and said: "Chuck, my friend, I am going to tell you the secret of life. First, the purpose of life is happiness. Second, happiness is like a house-fly. The more you chase it, the more it eludes you. You must learn to be still, like the waters of a frozen lake; then happiness will come and land on your nose."

I understood then why his eyes were crossed. He was looking for happiness.

Is that what we do? We sit and wait for happiness to find us? I don't think so. To be happy, we need to be in the process of meeting our goals. We may not meet all of them, but we will meet many of them and, along the road, we will be happy, because we are on the road. There is nothing more exciting than to have a constant supply of new ideas and opportunities.

The third statement, happiness is a state of mind, is literally true and about as useful as a cow in a vegan commune. This idea gives the impression that you can just sit and be happy, like my cross-eyed friend. Where is the instruction manual for achieving this blissful state of mind?

Finally, we turn to that all important "take life by the horns" statement: Happiness is a decision you make.

I have met many people who respond to that with everything from amusement to open hostility. "I am supposed to just get up in the morning and decide to be happy. Thanks. What do I owe you for that advice?"

If you are a therapist or counselor, I bet you have heard that retort more than once. I'm betting also that you were stuck for what to say in return.

What if we change the words to: Happiness is a commitment to yourself to get the things you want in life.

I'm willing to bet that everyone reading this has some things they want which they are not working on getting. That's depressing. What if you change the way you do life? What if you decide today, to make a list of the things you want and start working on them?

Happiness is a commitment to yourself to get the things you want in life.

You already do this to some extent. You buy things. You go on vacation. You change jobs. You start a new relationship. As we noted before, getting those things makes you happy for a while. Then the happiness wears off and you start trying to get something else to make you happy.

The reason that the happiness wears off is that happiness does not come from the thing you get, it comes from the commitment to yourself that you will get it. I assert, I believe, I preach that a life of commitment is a happy life. To have commitment, you need goals. To have goals, you have to admit what you want.

So you will not think that I'm preaching the gospel of greed and self-absorption, let me say that "what you want" may include helping others, working for social change, or any act of kindness that you can think of. As we get older, our wants often turn from meeting our needs to helping others meet theirs.

> *I assert, I believe, I preach that a life of commitment is a happy life.*

The key is that it is what you want, not what you think you should want or have to do. True commitment comes from desire not from obligation. Marshall Rosenberg expresses this idea in his book, *Non-Violent Communication: A Language of Life.* See "Why We Do What We Do" in the appendices.

I recently had lunch with a friend who was dieting, one of the most common "have to's" in the United States. She brought a bag of carrots, celery and apples. While I munched my slice of pizza, I asked her how her carrots were.

> *True commitment comes from desire not from obligation.*

"Just fine," she replied, eyeing my slice of pizza. "If you really want to know, I'd rather have that slice of pizza."

"I'll bet you have a sense of satisfaction that you are sticking to your diet," I offered, wanting to be supportive.

"True," she said, "but could you please cut me one bite of that pizza?"

How many carrot sticks does it take to satisfy the craving for a bite of pizza?

I cut her a small bite of my pizza. She ate it with her eyes closed, chewing slowly, savoring the taste. Then she finished her lunch of rabbit food. Sometimes, a commitment to a goal, in this case dieting, just needs a little bite of happiness.

What Goals Are

Here are My Goals

So that you will know that I practice what I preach, here is my current (as I write this) list of goals. These are long term goals.

- *Write and self publish a book on fear, anxiety and setting goals*
- *Write a novel and get it published*
- *Explore new aspects of working with others to be less worried and happier*
- *Rekindle my love for ballroom dancing*
- *Meanwhile, enjoy the ride*

Each of these goals has many ETs (Enabling Tasks) that need to be set to achieve them. For example, goal three might have ETs like "design a group for people who are stuck or on the brink of a life transition."

As you look at my goals, you may be thinking, *those first three seem reasonably clear. Those last two are vague.* That is observant of you. "Meanwhile, enjoy the ride" is purposely vague and I will discuss it in a few paragraphs. "Rekindle my love for ballroom dancing" it is a gutless goal. I will tell you why in the section below, "What Do You Want."

Goal setting is about deciding what you want in your life, now and in the future. Goal setting is about where you're going to direct you energy—how you're going to spend your time.

True Goals are Win-Win Situations

Working on the goals contributes to happiness. That doesn't mean working on a goal is all fun.

Writing a novel is good example. I have been writing since I was a teenager: poems, short stories, essays, articles, and most recently blogging. I have had some work published. I am good at nonfiction. I've never written a novel, and I'm still learning how.

I have written short stories. I know the basics of plot, character, voice, theme, and all the other elements of fiction. I don't yet have the skills to use them in a novel length story.

Writing and publishing a novel is going to involve pain, learning new things, and taking a risk in letting people read and critique my work. After I have made my best effort, there is luck involved in getting a novel published. Commitment carries risk for pain and disappointment. I repeat: *It's not about what you can do; it's about what you want to do.*

Many things about working on a novel are fun and make me happy. I write short stories and submit to contests. It can be exciting, part of "enjoying the ride."

Meanwhile, Enjoy the Ride

You may wonder what that last goal means and why I include it.

Your goals must include the daily enjoyment of life. "Enjoy the ride" means that while I'm working my goals, I do a lot of fun stuff. Studies of successful people show that they achieve long term goals by delaying gratification. They can live without the big payday long enough to get to the big payday.

One key strategy for doing this is to have little payoffs along the way. Build into your daily goals, the things you do for fun. If you leave fun out of your goals, you are, as they say, screwed.

I believe you will find that if you set goals for the things you most want, working on them will be fun even when it's not fun. Writing is fun. Rewriting is not as much fun. Editing is not fun at all. Yet, when I was rewriting and editing the drafts of this book, I had trouble getting myself away from the computer. It was not fun, but it was where my energy was. To experience this flow of energy, you have to get in touch with what you want.

What Do You Want?

I'm amazed at how often I hear from people who say they don't know what they want. If you're not sure what you want, you need to ask your "Self." The dialogue might go like this.

You: So, what do you want?

Self: I don't know.

You: What do you mean you don't know?

Self: Never thought about it.

You: That's why I asked. Think about it.

Self: Well, an Italian Beef for lunch would be nice.

That may be as far as you get the first time you ask your Self what you want. What keeps us from acknowledging what we want? Let's return to that gutless goal I mentioned.

My Gutless Goal

I started learning partner dancing (ballroom, Latin, swing, country) back in 2001. I made a commitment to myself that I was going to become a good social dancer. I think I accomplished that goal and, over the years, dancing has been a large piece of my social life.

If you have watched "Dancing With the Stars," you know that there is another kind of dancing. Couples, on that show, are performing a pattern of prepared steps to a particular piece of music. In the dancing world, this is often called a "showcase" dance. It differs from social dancing in that the object is to entertain others. I have never done a showcase. Yet, every time I watch couples doing showcases, I am envious.

Recall the first two steps of goal setting: acknowledge and actuate. This is what makes a goal real and it creates the commitment needed to follow through. If you don't acknowledge what you want, you can't expect to achieve it.

We have a Self that knows what we want. We also have an Ego that gets in the way of what we want because our Ego is there to protect us. It tries to make sure we don't feel uncomfortable, unsafe, embarrassed, or insecure. In short, it protects us from risk.

My Self knows that I want to learn and perform a showcase. My Ego shoots my Self down. The dialogue, in my head, goes like this. Imagine that I am watching a couple do a showcase.

Self: That would be so much fun to do.
Ego: Yeah, but he just messed up, nearly tripped.
Self: So what. Nobody cares if they're not perfect.
Ego: You'd be really embarrassed if you didn't do it perfectly.
Self: Maybe I will find a teacher to help me be a better dancer.
Ego: You don't have time. You have no idea how many hours of practice it takes.
Self: I don't know. Maybe you're right.

Does this dialogue sound familiar? Have you ever wanted to do something and shot yourself down? Our Ego's interest is in protecting us from unpleasant feelings. Anything we do that is hard will have some unpleasant feelings. So our Egos have a lot of power over us.

You may be asking how we can *really know* that we want to do something. The answer is that we listen to our Self. *My Self is speaking to me though my feelings of envy when I watch other people do a showcase.*

You may be rolling your eyes by this point and saying, "All right, why doesn't your goal list say: "learn and perform a showcase?"

I respond: So far, my Ego is winning the debate. I know what I want; I am scaring myself about doing it. Maybe it will take too much of my time. Maybe it will be too hard. What if I don't do it well? What if I don't dance like Fred Astaire?

> *We have two reasons why we don't do something: a good reason and the real reason.*

When it comes to acknowledging what we want, we have two reasons why we don't to something: a good reason and the real reason.

All those fears about not having time, not being perfect, making mistakes — they are all good reasons for not learning to perform a showcase. None of them are the real reason.

The real reason is that I don't have the self-image of a dancer. I look at good male dancers. I see how they move; how they are not afraid to express themselves with their movements. I feel like a klutz when I watch.

Could I move like that, I ask myself. *What kind of change in my self-image would that take? What would it feel like?*

To do something extraordinary almost always requires a change in our self-image, how we look at ourselves, and ultimately how others look at us. I think that is what often holds us back.

Look out there in the world. What makes you envious? Maybe it's hearing someone play an instrument, watching a great golfer make a hard putt, or reading a well written story or novel. How would you feel about yourself if you could do that? How would it change you? How would others look at you?

How would I feel if I could dance like Fred Astaire?

"Hold the phone," says my Ego. "You need to seriously lower your expectations.

Better to be a nice safe social dancer. You dance better than you ever expected now. You are just fine."

See how well our Egos protect us from risk?

When is the last time you had an honest talk between your Self and your Ego? What is your Ego keeping you from doing? How do you get your Self to speak louder than your Ego?

You unchain your unconscious.

Unchaining Your Unconscious

Remember that I said: You know what you want.

To be more accurate, your unconscious mind knows what you want. For our purposes, the unconscious mind includes everything that goes on in your head that you are not conscious of at the moment. Processes that are unconscious include:

- *Speaking your native language (we are only conscious of the intent to speak)*
- *Riding a bicycle (once it becomes second nature)*
- *Recalling a phone number (you have the conscious intent to recall it; the process of recall in not conscious)*
- *Liking the taste of chocolate (you are conscious of it tasting good but the evaluation of its taste is unconscious)*

Most of what happens in our heads is unconscious. What you want is rattling around in there someplace. You need to find it.

How do you tap your unconscious? The mere intention to do so is the first step. Your conscious mind (Con) gives instructions to your unconscious mind (Uncon). Do you ever say things like:

- *I could never do that*
- *That will never happen*
- *I don't have time for that*

When you say such things, your unconscious mind hears and believes what you say. We Con our Uncon into believing what we can or can't do. Our Uncon follows our orders. This truth has been known by sages and mystics throughout the ages.

You may have received negative messages like this from your parents or other authority figures. Children internalize what adults tell them. If they are told that what they want is impossible, or not good for them, or is something they don't deserve, they accept it. From there it's an easy step to "I don't know what I want" because it is better not to know than to know and think you can't have it or don't deserve it.

These children have been "Conned" and they go right on Conning themselves about what they want. Stop Conning. The TRUTH is: You know what you want.

Individuals who meditate or pray practice speaking and listening to the unconscious mind. Used by athletes, musicians, writers, entrepreneurs, and successful people in general, the practices of meditating and praying are known pathways to the unconscious mind.

> *The TRUTH is: You know what you want.*

Another way to the unconscious is to focus on what you want to do. Golfers, for example, know that when they focus on where they want the ball to go, they hit the ball more accurately. Think the result and you achieve the result.

Every time you think or say a negative message, you focus in the wrong direction. The first step to releasing your unconscious desires is to tell your unconscious that you want to know what it knows about you that you don't know. Here are a few basic techniques for doing that:

- *Give yourself "I can, I will" messages*
- *Keep a journal of thoughts and feelings that you have about your future*
- *Keep a dream journal*
- *Start setting small goals today; the bigger ones will come to you later*
- *Start setting a time aside each day for prayer or meditation (20 minutes is enough)*
- *Listen to the your fleeting thoughts and feelings. Write them in your journal.*

I call these fleeting thoughts "flash fantasies." They go through the mind in an instant. The envy I feel when watching a showcase is a good example. I think these fleeting thoughts and feelings are your Uncon talking to you, much like dreams. Write them down. Some people carry a little notebook for this purpose.

From the process of unchaining your unconscious, you will start to identify what you want to do with your life in, say, the next two to five years. Some of these will become your goals. You might be asking, "Is everything I want a goal?" Let's talk about what goals are not.

What Goals Are Not

Goals Are Not a To-Do List

I have am too busy to do To-Do lists. Many people make endless To-Do lists and all they get is more anxious about what they have to do. See the Appendices for a suggestion about what you can do with your To-Do list.

A To-Do list, whether on paper or in your head, is a list of the trivia you need to get done. Some of it may be important: pay the rent, buy toilet paper, and call your mother. Some of it is may be time suckers: clean up the garage, reorganize your CD collection. We all have time suckers on our To-Do lists, whether they are on paper or in our head.

To-Do's are not about giving your life more meaning, unless you include tasks that are relevant to achieving your goals. Those are the tasks that should be on your daily goal list. Goals are not about getting stuff done; they are about making your life a better place to live in.

> *Goals are not about getting stuff done; They are about making your life a better place to live in.*

"Shoulds" Are Not Goals

Your current goals are things you're working on. You cannot work on everything you want all at the same time. The trick is to work on goals that give you a sense of meaning and purpose and are where your emotional energy is.

When you think about a goal, what words do you hear in your head? If you hear "I want to find a better job," that may be a goal. If what you hear is "I should get a better job," it's probably not a goal. To make this distinction clearer, use the following exercise:

You: What do you want?
Self: I should get a better job.
You: Is that important to you?
Self: Sure.
You: Why is that important?
Self: Well, I could make more money.
You: Why is making more money important?

Self: I could go on more vacations, stuff like that.

You: You want to go on more vacations?

Self: Damn Straight!

You: What is your goal?

Self: I want to go on more vacations.

Beneath a "should," there may be a "want." You need to find the "want." The "should" will not get you there. "Shoulds" have no emotional energy in them. All your emotional energy is in your wants.

You can achieve a "Should" goal, but it will not be much fun and it won't make your life much happier or meaningful. Imagine the person above. She gets a better job, works harder, makes more money. She has less time for vacations. There is the irony. When we pursue a "Should" goal, we often ignore what we want.

> *All your emotional energy is in your wants.*

> *It is not about what you SHOULD do;*
> *It is about what you WANT to do.*

Find the "Want" beneath the "Should" and then pursue the "Want."

The Four Rules of Project Management

Rule One: Is the Juice Worth the Squeeze?

How important is your goal? What if you count the costs and the benefit is not there? We often keep the "I want to date Angelina Jolie" goals in our heads for years and never take a single step toward doing them.

We do that because it is safer than setting our sights on something we want and can get. We avoid the risk and the hard work. Part of setting goals is letting go of goals that are not worth the cost to us.

What happens when it is something we do want but we can't imagine getting it or think we don't deserve it. What if the *juice is worth the squeeze*, but the squeeze is going to involve huge cost, a long effort, and risk?

Remember when a friend confided in you about something they want to do. They seemed to want advice and yet nothing you said helped. The conversation may have sounded like this.

Friend: I'm thinking about going back for my master's.

You: Wow, that's exciting.

Friend: Yeah, it's expensive too; about thirty thousand.

You: Hey, there are student loans.

Friend: And work is so busy right now.

You: Tell your boss you want to get your master's. Maybe he'll cut you some slack?

Friend: Are you kidding? Old nose-to-the-grindstone George?

You: Maybe you could do it part-time.

Friend: Then it would take forever.

Your friend may have concluded the conversation with "Boy, you're no help," This left you angry and her feeling vindicated. She has proven that she can't get what she wants.

Your friend is not making excuses to be difficult. Her Ego is telling her that she can't get or doesn't deserve the thing she wants. Her self-image is not letting her see her Self as someone with a master's degree. Our self-image usually lags behind our needs and wants.

The conversation above is an example of what Dr. Eric Berne called

"Why Don't You — Yes But." (Yes-But, for short), first described in his book *Games People Play*. The purpose of this game is to get the listener to try to solve your problem, and then shoot down all the solutions. The result is to confirm your belief that you can't get what you want. This is a major way our Egos protect us from doing something we perceive as risky.

When someone Yes-Buts you, giving them advise will not help them. If fact, you are helping them dig further into their fears and doubts. How do you talk to someone who wants to play Yes-But with you? The answer is: focus on getting them to acknowledge what they want or need. Stay with that. Do not offer advice.

> Friend: I'm thinking about going back for my master's.
> You: Wow, that's exciting.
> Friend: Yeah, it's expensive too; about thirty thousand.
> You: It would be worth it.
> Friend: And work is so busy right now.
> You: You have said many times, you are bored with your job.
> Friend: Bored is better than unemployed.
> You: It sounds like a really tough decision but I'd love to attend your graduation.

This conversation will go one of two ways. Either your friend will get frustrated that you are not playing the game, or maybe the friend will start thinking about how to get this need met. Either way, you do not take on their frustration.

We also play Yes-But with ourselves. When you find you are playing Yes-But with yourself, the same rule applies. Don't give yourself advice. Stop trying to figure out how to meet your need or goal and just acknowledge its existence. Feel your need. We play Yes-But, because we're avoiding taking the actions needed to get what we want.

The "actions" might include spending the money, telling the boss you need time off, or juggling work and school. If the goal isn't impor-

> *We play Yes-But, because we're avoiding taking the actions needed to get what we want.*

tant, then let it go. The juice may not be worth the squeeze. If you want that master's degree, that expensive vacation, that new career, then make it a goal. Acknowledge what is crucial to your happiness. When you have done that, your unconscious mind will go to work and figure out how to get it.

Rule Two: Things Change

I spent thirty years in information technology designing and writing computer systems and later designing and leading projects. The second rule of project management is "Things change." What we want doesn't stay the same and the path to getting it usually doesn't stay the same.

As I was writing this book, I started another project. I wanted to re-place the carpeting on the floor of my storage room with easier-to-clean tile. I moved everything, including my cat's litter box, into my second bedroom and tore up the carpet. The project then sat for three weeks because I was determined to get the first draft of this book done.

While revising the first draft, I was thinking more and more about getting the storage room done. My internal parent said: *You have to get this book done.*

I sat there, gritting my teeth, revising the draft, while my mind was re-ally thinking about the storage room. After a while, I was rushing through the writing so I could get to the storage room.

Finally, I gave in to that inner voice that said my priorities had taken a detour, and I started spending part of my time on the storage room.

Second Rule of Project Management:
THINGS CHANGE!

Even when you have a list of goals that are important to you, you need to listen to the inner voice that sets your priorities. Where is your energy? If you ignore your energy, your forward motion will stop. Once I had a plan for getting the storage room done, which involved getting someone else to do the work, my brain was ready to focus on writing again.

Rule Three: Do the Next Right Thing

I used to tell people that my job as a project manager was to make sure that the project team was doing "the next right thing."

That may be the next step on your project plan and it may not be. A plan is a map that keeps you accountable to your goals. It is not a straight-jacket.

Third Rule of Project Management:
Do the next right thing.

You probably have goals on your list that you are working on at the same time. What do you work on this morning? Refer to the third rule of project management. What tells you what the next right thing is? Where is your energy today? If it's in writing, then write, if it's in laying down new tile, then do that.

I make you a promise. If you go where your energy is telling you to go, this day, this minute, you will achieve your goals. If you fight your energy, you will spin your wheels.

That brings us to the fourth and final rule of project management

Rule Four: Plan the Work, Work the Plan

Goals can be short-term or long-term.

I already gave you some examples of my long-term goals. Long-term goals are those that take more than one month and usually require enabling tasks (ETs). Why one month? One month is the longest time most people can focus on a single task and do it or know they didn't do it. For perspective, a short-term goal might be "Clean my condo."

If you are not a cleaner, then your condo/apartment/house probably needs some cleaning. How many hours does it take to do that? Let us say four hours. How many days will it take you to devote four hours to cleaning? It ought to be less than a month. After a month, if you still haven't done the cleaning, you probably need to reassess the goal. You may be chasing a "Should" goal.

If you decide it is a "Want to" goal, then maybe it needs to become a longer-term goal. Then you need to break it down; give it some ETs. Possible Enabling Tasks for Cleaning My Condo are:

- *Vacuum the carpet bimonthly*
- *Clean the big bathroom weekly*
- *Clean the little bathroom biweekly.*

The purpose of ETs is to break down a large goal. Most goals that last for more than a month need ETs. Another reason for using ETs is when the goal is vague. Parents with children who have attention problems know that "Clean your room" is a useless instruction. They have to say, "Pick up your cloths and put them in the laundry. After that, get all the leftover food out from under you bed."

For some people, "Clean my Condo" is clear and manageable. However, if you are like me, I could look at that goal for six months and it would never motivate me to do anything.

For me, "Clean My Condo" will never be anything but a "Should" goal. It will never have any energy. I am what I call an "entropy housekeeper." Remember "entropy" from high school physics?

Entropy is the tendency of the universe to move from order to chaos. When something in my condo is in sufficient chaos, I clean. That means

I do my dishes every day, well, almost every day. I vacuum about once a month, maybe.

For this kind of goal to work, I need it broken into manageable pieces and I need major incentives. Incentives will be addressed in the next section on Rewards.

Breaking long-term goals into ETs is how you implement the fourth rule of project management:

Fourth Rule of Project Management:
Plan the work; work the plan.

Long-term goals can have time frames beyond one month and up to many years. I peg my "write a novel and get it published' to about five years. The writing won't take that long. What takes time is the practice, feedback, and revision needed to create a long story. The task list for this goal would look like the project plans I did as a project leader in Information Management. Some of the ETs might be:

- *Get an idea for the novel (done)*
- *Write single sentence summary (done)*
- *Write three act summary (in progress)*
- *Write the back-stories of each main character (in progress)*
- *Write a scene summary for the story*
- *Write the first chapter of the novel*
- *Read other people's novels*
- *Read other people's writing advice*
- *Practice writing something everyday*
- *Find a reader group to read my work and show me theirs*
- *Attend at least one writer's conference*

You get the idea. What I have listed above might be the first six months of the process. Some tasks are going to happen at the same time.

The important thing is any long-term goal needs a project plan. The plan holds you accountable. It also rewards you for progress. As you check off completed ETs, you will have a sense of "doing it" that will make you feel good and create momentum.

ETs will make up the content of your day-to-day goal list, which consists of goals that can be done in one month.

Keeping Yourself on Track

Rewards

A study was done a few years ago to find out why some students do well in school and others do not. The researchers went to grade school classes and made the following offer.

I have some candy bars here. You can have one candy bar today or two candy bars tomorrow. They noted which kids took a candy bar today and which waited until tomorrow.

Then they tracked their grades for several years.

I probably don't have to tell you that the students that waited until tomorrow for two candy bars had better grade records. I'm also sure that you can guess the reason. Young people who can wait to get something better, called "delaying gratification," are able to put off watching TV or playing a video game until their homework is done.

To delay gratification, you have to see the reward coming. What if they had said to those grade-schoolers, "You can have one candy bar today or two candy bars next week." I doubt many would have waited that long.

Your rewards must appeal to your emotional energy today. Usually that means the reward can't be too far in the future. If you are going to get out of bed every morning and jog for forty-five minutes to get into shape, the reward of fitting into a smaller dress or pants size in six months probably will not motivate you. I want my reward now or very soon.

An example of a reward might be: *If I wake up and jog every day this week for forty-five minutes, then on Saturday I get to shop for that new dress or pair of pants.* Can you wait until Saturday for your candy bars? The key is that a reward must affect your emotional energy today.

"But," you say, "achieving a goal *should* be a reward all by itself."

> *A reward must affect your emotional energy today.*

There's that word "should" again. It has no place in a rational discussion of human behavior. We should do all kinds of things. There is no energy in should. Someone once said that all the "shoulds" in the world and twenty-five cents will buy you a cup of coffee. He said it a long time ago.

The problem is that the reward of achieving a long-term goal is often too far off. It will motivate us part of the time, but it especially won't motivate us when we are doing the parts of the long term goal that are tedious or painful. Think about jogging on those mornings when you wake with an ache or stiffness, or it's raining. Your reward has to motivate you in face of such obstacles. Which reminds me: *All goal lists must include play.*

Play means "what is in it for me *today?*" Go back to "Clean my Condo." How do I make that into play? You turn it from a "Should" goal to a "Want to" goal? You could create a reward for "Clean my condo." How about "invite four people over for dinner on the third Saturday of the month." That ought to get you moving. The day of your dinner party, you will be cleaning like mad.

> *The test is that when you think about the reward, you get excited, happy, you feel good, and you look forward to it.*

This assumes that entertaining is rewarding to you. If not, then think of something else. The litmus test is that when you think about the reward, you get excited, happy, you feel good, and you look forward to it. "Won't my mother be proud of me if I clean my condo" is probably not a reward for most of us.

For some people, having a clean house is a reward by itself. For the rest of us, we must have rewards for the grueling labor of running a vacuum sweeper. You need something in it for you other than "I should do it."

Our inner motivation for what we do determines the energy we put into doing something. In his book, *Non-Violent Communication: A Language of Life*, Marshall Rosenberg says "I earnestly believe, however, that an important form of self-compassion is to make choices motivated purely by our desire to contribute to life, rather than out of fear, guilt, shame, duty, or obligation"

You can read more about "shoulds," self-criticism, and self-compassion in Chapter Nine of Dr. Rosenberg's book. See also "Why We Do What we Do" in the appendices of this book.

Your Day-to-Day Goal List

I have shared my longest term goals so you can see the "scale" of large goals. Some of these goals will stretch more than a month and have been broken into ETs that can be achieved in a month. You break long term goals into enabling tasks that are themselves short-term goals. Your short-term goals and enabling tasks are your day-to-day goal list.

Your Goal/ET list will change regularly and needs to be posted in several places in your home: over your desk, in the kitchen, in the bathroom. A good place is over your television set or wherever else you tend to go to escape your life. We want your life to be your

> *If your goals are not more exciting to you than watching TV, you need to rethink your goals.*

excitement, your entertainment, your refuge from stress. If your goals are not more exciting to you than watching TV, you need to rethink your goals.

This is what my current goal sheet looks like. They aren't numbered because their relative importance is not important. They are all things I'm working on now. I have marked the ETs. I show ballpark time frames for some goals. You will also notice that I show revisions or leave goals on the list after they are done, providing a sense of achievement and forward motion.

Day-To-Day Goals

- *Write a Second draft of "Are You Wishing Your Life Away" (ET-2 weeks)*
- *Start a support group to help people deal with anxiety and set goals (Needs ETs)*
- *Enter short story "Seeds" in contest (Done – yeh! – Crap! – Didn't win.)*
- *Finish short story "Blood Spots" (Done)*
- *Enter "Blood Spots" in contest (1 week)*
- *Finish 3 act summary of novel (ET-no current progress – revise goal)*
- *Take Viennese Waltz   Country-Two Step*
- *Viennese Waltz Lesson weekly (ET)*
- *Enjoy the summer!*

First, note that my "Gutless Goal," about ballroom dancing, results in a lack of commitment in setting an enabling task. I can't even decide what dance to focus on. How can you plan how to achieve something, when you are not admitting that you want it in the first place?

Notice also what you do not see on this goal list: do the laundry, pay the electric bill, or do the tax numbers for accountant. Those are To-Dos. They may be important things to get done; they are not goals. Goals are actions that excite you and give your life meaning.

> *Goals are actions that excite you and give your life meaning.*

What Do You Do Now?

You have unchained your unconscious and you should now be looking at a list of goals that are your dreams. You have assigned ballpark time frames and decided on the first ET for each long-term goal. You have written a day-to-day goal list. Everything on that list should be do-able in one month or less.

Now what?

You start working on your goal list. You start telling people about your goals. You get excited about your goals. If excitement doesn't happen, go back to the beginning:

It's not about what you can or should do; it's about what you WANT to do. How many times do I have to tell you that?

Here are some possible snags:

- *The number of items on your day-to-day goal list exceeds what you can do in one month.*
- *You find that after two weeks, you have a goal, on the list that you are not working toward.*
- *You find yourself sitting at your computer looking up "How to make a Tofu Quiche" or "solder copper pipe" and realize you don't have a goal for that.*

The first two snags are "no brainers," as they used to say in my old field of project management. You may have too many items on your list and need to prioritize. Priorities are something corporations devote considerable time to.

Business people make lists of projects they want the computer geeks to work on. When the geeks ask them which one they want done first, they say, "All of them." Each person's pet project is the number-one priority.

You have control over what *you* do first, second, third. How do you decide? Go back to Rule 2: *Do the next right thing.* What tells you the next right thing? Where is your energy? What do you think about? That is the next right thing.

The solution for snags one and two is cut and revise your list and this time express what your energy is telling you to work on.

Snag three is a bit more complicated and the one you will struggle with constantly. Partly, it is about setting the goals you really want to work on and partly it is about your need to avoid working on them. The solution is to make sure there is fun built into your goals.

Include Enjoyment Goals

When I first started keeping a list of my goals, posted on my walls in three places, I had a problem. Sometimes I wasn't doing anything that supported my goals. I'd surf the web looking up "cosmic string theory," and I'd ask my Self, "Self, how is this supporting my goals?" If I spend ten minutes doing this, maybe the question isn't so important. How about if I have spent four hours doing it?

There is one goal on my list that browsing the Internet could come under: "Enjoy the summer." Am I enjoying looking for this piece of information on the Internet? If I am, okay. If not, get on with "enjoying the summer." How about going for a ride on my bike? *Fun is so important!*

How many times have you heard people say things like, "Boy, the summer's over. Seems like it just started." They mean, "The summer is almost over and I haven't enjoyed it." Fun is a major emotional need. Ignore it at your peril.

> *Fun is a major emotional need. Ignore it at your peril.*

That is why you need at least one pure enjoyment goal on your goal list. "What do I enjoy?" is an overlooked question to wake your consciousness.

Each day will tell me what "Enjoy the summer" means.

- *Ride my bike*
- *Take walks in the evening.*
- *Eat at outdoor restaurants*
- *Go to the water park*

Identify the things you enjoy. Make it a goal to do them more and stop doing the time suckers that steal your time and energy.

Major Goals – Your Commitment Statement

Long-term goals are those the take more than a month. Major goals are those that will take a year or more to complete. They could include going back to school for a new degree, remodeling your kitchen (when you do not have the money yet) or planning a European vacation for next year.

Major goals require ETs to help you take the necessary steps to get them done. They also require serious commitment because there are going to be roadblocks and distractions along the way.

To get you past the distractions and roadblocks, you need a commitment statement. My longest term goal, at the moment is to write and publish a novel. Here is my commitment statement:

My Commitment on Writing a Novel
I will write and publish a novel. I am going to do this because
I have the ability to do it and because it will contribute to my

happiness and sense of purpose. I'm going to do it because I have
clever ideas for novels and it is time I start sharing them. I will
do it because the idea of entertaining people, making them laugh
or cry, sends goose bumps through me. I so need to do this.
I refuse to let anything get in my way.

(The idea of using a commitment statement came from *Writing Fiction for Dummies* by Randy Ingermanson and Peter Economy (2009))

Write your statement in your handwriting or type it if you prefer. Either way, make it personal. Date and sign it. Post copies where you will see them and where others will see them.

You can include a time commitment if you have a realistic idea of how long it will take to do this goal. Otherwise leave it out. I do not have a good feel for how long it will take to write and publish a novel. Since I have considerable learning to do, I'm guessing five years. Maybe it will take less than that, maybe more.

I want you to look carefully at the last sentence of my commitment statement. I call this the "no-wiggle" clause: "I refuse to let anything get in my way." It's the most important sentence in the commitment statement. When I decided to go back to school, to get a master's degree in counseling, and open a private counseling practice, I knew that there would be huge roadblocks. I had started law school back in the seventies and then quit. I didn't want to do that again.

When I returned to school for a master's in counseling, I made a firm, unalterable commitment to myself about what I intended to do. I also told a lot of other people. Since I suspected that opening a private practice would be the hardest part, I was particularly clear about declaring that as part of my goal.

During school, when we talked about our future plans in the counseling field, I said *I'm going to open a private practice.* I also told my friends, my family, and my co-workers at my old job.

Declaring that you will achieve a goal *no matter what* is powerful. It gets you past the moments of doubt about your decision. The strategy for achieving the goal can change, not the goal. If I had allowed myself wiggle room about this goal, there are a dozen places along the way that it would have been too easy to back out. I know many people who earned their master's degree in counseling and have never sat for their licensing examination. You can get a counseling job in an agency or hospital without a license. You cannot open a private practice in Illinois without a license.

There is nothing wrong with working for an agency or hospital, if that's what you want to do. That wasn't for me. My commitment had to include opening a practice. That's what I wanted. *Commitment is everything.*

Your Battle Plan

"No battle was ever won according to plan,
but no battle was ever won without one."
—*General Dwight Eisenhower*

General Eisenhower was saying that no plan works as you thought it would. The hallmark of good project planning is continuous replanning. Hostile forces are out there waiting to shoot you down. My first battle plan for changing careers looked like this:

- *Explore schools and choose where to apply*
- *Apply to schools*
- *Figure out how to work fulltime and go to school part-time*
- *Figure out how to pay for school (financial aid??)*
- *Start school*

- *Graduate*
- *Get licensed*
- *Open practice*
- *Live happily ever after*

You notice there wasn't much detail. The tasks up to "Graduate" I could flesh out. "Get licensed" was another thing altogether.

I had looked up the state licensing requirements. I couldn't pick a school or curriculum without knowing I would graduate with the necessary course work to meet the legal licensing criteria. I met other students who had not bothered to check this out. They trusted our school's marketing statements in their course catalogs. That is the difference between being twenty-two and being fifty-two. At fifty-two the rule is: trust but verify.

In Illinois, one of the licensing requirements for LCPC (Licensed Clinical Professional Counselor) candidates involves two years of fulltime supervised practice after graduating with a master's degree. I had no idea how hard it would be to get a job in an agency, especially at my age, in order to get that two years of experience.

Even before I got my master's hood during graduation at the Harold Washington Library in Chicago, I started job hunting. I set a goal of sending out two resumes a day, and was picky about the job I wanted. I focused on mental-health hospitals and social agencies within a twenty-mile radius. Six months and dozens of resumes later, I had not had a single interview. As a computer programmer, I was accustomed to getting interviews and job offers. Being ignored was shocking, discouraging, infuriating.

I spent hours on the computer, writing cover letters, revising my resume, making phone calls. I got nothing. I dreaded looking at the new job listings on Monster.com and Careerbuilder.com.

I was angry and tired. I felt defeated. My old field as a computer programmer and project leading was still paying the rent, not to mention bonuses, a 401K, good insurance, and vacations.

My morale was flagging. I wanted to retreat. What would be so wrong with working out my years to retirement? After that, I could do what I wanted. "Why am I changing careers anyway?" I asked my Self.

This is the most treacherous point in working toward a goal. You ask yourself the question: Why am I doing this? Do you want to answer this question when you are feeling defeated and discouraged? You could spend days and huge amounts of energy wrangling with that question. That is the purpose of the no-wiggle clause.

My no-wiggle clause came thundering onto my battlefield, like a cavalry charge. My Self answered, *"The question is irrelevant, immaterial, and evasive. This decision is not subject to review."*

I was especially angry with all those stupid, age discriminating, human resource idiots that wouldn't give me an interview. They were looking for two years' experience. I have experience in life, I shouted at the universe. See my gray hair?

The Four Horsemen of the Apocalypse were charging up the hill at me. Their names were Fear, Self-doubt, Disappointment, and Anger.

Chamberlain's Charge

On the second day of the Battle of Gettysburg, Colonel Joshua Lawrence Chamberlain's Union regiment was positioned at the far end of Cemetery Ridge. The Rebels had charged up the hill twice and Chamberlain's men had repelled them. Chamberlain knew there was daylight for one more charge and he suspected the Confederate forces would come at him again.

His regiment had taken heavy losses and they were out of ordinance. He had sent runners for more ammunition; they returned, reporting that, by some SNAFU, the ordinance wagons weren't positioned where they expected them. Chamberlain called together his officers and told them they couldn't withstand another charge by the enemy force. Neither could they fall back. If they did, the Rebel army would flank the Union army and get behind them.

He ordered his officers to have their men load their last rounds, affix bayonets and, on his order, charge *down the hill*. This was about as crazy an idea as his officers had ever heard, but they had grown to respect this quiet professor of rhetoric from Bowdoin College in Maine.

When the Confederate attack came, Chamberlain, with sword in one hand and pistol in the other, led his men down the hill, yelling and firing their last rounds. The Rebel soldiers were so surprised they broke and retreated in disarray.

Chamberlain's Charge, as it known by historians, saved the day and won Josh Chamberlain the Medal of Honor.

There I sat, at my computer, unable to hold my position, and unable to retreat. The remaining choice is to charge. I revised my resume, again. A friend suggested that I remove anything reflecting my age. She also suggested that, before my first interview, I color my hair to hide the gray.

I sent out twice the number of resumes, increased the area to forty miles, and made my only job requirement that I would get clinical experience and supervision to satisfy the licensing statute. It took six more months. In that time, I had about six interviews and a job offer. The job required a one-hour commute, and was not at all the kind of job I wanted. But the job would get me the experience and hours I needed for licensure.

I quit my $100,000 a year job in Information Technology and started a $32,000 a year job in mental health. *Commitment is everything.*

Holding Yourself Accountable

Claiming you have a commitment is easy. Actually having one is not. I have two married friends. I will call them Arthur and Gwen. Arthur and Gwen are devout Christians. They are among the few people I know who walk the talk about their beliefs. For Arthur and Gwen, there is no divorce statute. When they said, "until death do us part," they meant it.

While in graduate school I interviewed them for a class assignment. They talked about their marriage and how their religious beliefs informed their lives as a couple. I asked them if they argue. They laughed and Gwen told me *"arguing shapes the relationship and helps people learn about one another."*

The problem, Arthur said, is that when "winning the argument" is more important than learning about each other, the argument becomes about power. I will never forget what he said next, *"There is no victory in defeating a woman that you know you will spend the rest of your life with."* Commitment shapes how we do things.

> *Commitment shapes how we do things.*

Most people want to be confident in a decision before they commit themselves. This is why thinking things through and doing some homework before deciding an action is a good idea.

For many people, "being confident" means having no doubts, but no serious decision comes without doubts. The mysterious fact is that once you have committed, doubts are no longer important. Doubts are a bump in the daily road to reaching your goal, fulfilling your commitment. Waiting until you have no doubts before you make a commitment is a way to avoid making a commitment. You make the commitment to do something. Then you deal with your doubts.

> *How it works:*
> *You make the commitment to do something. Then you deal with your doubts.*

Tell People About Your Goals

I cannot emphasize enough how important it is to tell people what your goals are. A secret goal has a built in loophole. No one knows I ever intended to do this, so I can decide not to do it.

When people know about your goals, they are going to ask you the dreaded question: "How's that book going, Chuck?"

That question in going to be uncomfortable if you have been spending your time looking up how to make a Tofu Quiche. People know I am writing this book. They ask how it's going. That makes me uncomfortable when I'm not progressing. I want to say, "I finished the third draft" or, "I got the cover art back from the artist."

Where do I want to be with it at the end of next week? When do I want it published as an ebook? Have I started a group yet to help people with their goals? When am I going to do that? That's called "Accountability."

As a project leader in the corporate world, my boss held me accountable for my timeline. When people made time commitments to me, I held them accountable. Every meeting ended with the designated note taker, usually the person who called the meeting, writing action assignments. Action assignments are a list of what people commit to do and when they agree to get it done.

One of the business gurus of the 1980's, Tom Peters, wrote, "What gets measured, gets done." By setting goals and time frames and letting people know what you intend, you are measuring your progress. Without accountability, our lives drift from one thing to another.

Teenagers move from one thing to the next because it is a stage in their development where they explore their identity. Adults sometimes go through this stage again at midlife. They explore things to reexamine what they want in the later years of their lives. This is healthy.

You may find that you are in this exploration phase. If so, then your interests may change frequently, like a teenager. You goal becomes: explore my options. These include: going back to school, learning to play the Sitar, and moving to Buenos Aires. In this case, you may not want to advertise these things as goals because they're not goals yet. What you tell people is, "I'm exploring my options."

Can you change a goal once you have committed yourself to it? You can do whatever you want. Only you know whether you're copping out, or making a new decision, realigning and setting a better goal. Actuating your goal by telling other people what you intend to do will keep you honest at moments of self-doubt.

Being in Charge of Your Life

Think about 911. The people who lost their lives that day got up that morning thinking they had time. They had years to achieve their dreams.

You will probably not be the victim of a terrorist attack. But how many other things can cut your life short? Even more important, if you're not working on your dreams today, *what the hell are you doing?*

You build a dream by taking one step at a time. These steps are your goals. They are what your life is about. They're the steps to your happiness. You don't have to see the whole staircase, just take the first step.

You can't get everything you want in life, but you can get most of it. Moving toward what you want will make every day an opportunity, a new chance. I have friends who embrace Buddhist philosophy, and I admire their thinking. Yoga and meditation are widely accepted as excellent ways to relax, explore self, and grow.

> *If you're not working on your dreams today, what the hell are you doing?*

When these friends start telling me that they're working on "becoming enlightened" and letting go of all those things they think they want and need, that's where I respectfully disagree.

We are organic physical beings, at least on this plane of existence. We want what we want. We have needs and desires and dreams and hopes.

Predicating your happiness on getting everything you want is a recipe for unhappiness. On the other hand, to me, working on what you want while never letting go of today, never forgetting that tomorrow is a probability, not a certainty, is a good formula for contentment and happiness.

How do you want to walk this Earth?

Do you want to continue to be fearful or anxious? Or, do you want to walk with a confident grin and a bit of what-the-hell attitude? If you are wishing your life away, dreaming about what you might have done, telling yourself what you want is too hard, too risky, I implore you to stop. Risk taking is life giving.

Please give yourself more life.

Appendices: More About Anxieties and Goals

I made a commitment to keep this book short, so you can read it quickly and get on with your goals. I could have included many topics, and many of those have been covered in a host of other books. However, since some of these topics may be important to certain readers I've moved them to appendices.

The Threat Circuit

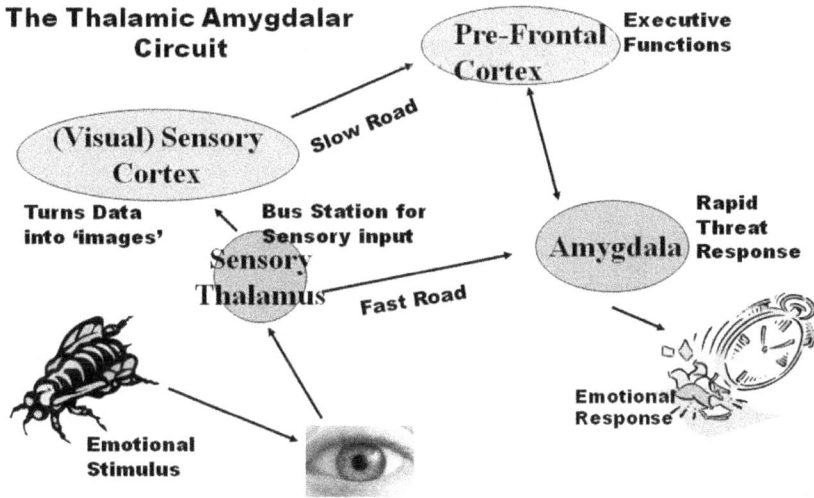

The Thalamic Amygdalar Circuit

Pre-Frontal Cortex — Executive Functions

(Visual) Sensory Cortex — Slow Road

Turns Data into 'images'

Bus Station for Sensory input

Sensory Thalamus — Fast Road

Amygdala — Rapid Threat Response

Emotional Stimulus

Emotional Response

When we experience something that might be a threat, the amygdala responds more quickly than our executive functions (the Slow Road). We sense that something is wrong even before we consciously see the possible threat (the Fast Road). This accounts for why our hand may jerk quickly away from a bug. It's as if we did not consciously move our hand. The diagram above is based on my understanding of some of the material discussed in Chapter 6 of The Emotional Brain by Joseph LeDoux. This diagram does not appear as shown in his book.

Simple Strategies for Fear and Anxiety

I promised you some cognitive and behavioral strategies for managing anxiety. Cognitive means you do it in your head. Behavioral means you change your behavior. They work together. If I change my thinking, I hope my behavior will change. If I change my behavior, I hope my thinking will change.

Many strategies exist for managing fear and anxiety. They take time to be effective because your brain is not an abstract object. It is a physical device with trillions of connections. As brain researcher, Joseph LeDoux, author of *Synaptic Self* says, we are the sum of connections (synapses) between the cells in our brains. Reprogramming these connections takes time and repetition, just as it takes time and practice to unlearn any habit and replace it with a new habit.

I want to provide you with a few simple ideas for managing anxieties.

Four strategies covered here are:
Just Stop!
Mindfulness
Reframing
Targeting your FEAR

Strategy 1: Just Stop!

"Just Stop" is my favorite because it is so simple. I use is so often it has become almost automatic. Anxiety is provoked by thoughts. Unless there is a car heading straight for you or a tiger is about to eat you, your thoughts are creating the anxiety. So stop thinking that thought. Here is how it works.

Suppose you are going to a party and you are thinking, "What if I go to the party and no one talks to me?" Just Stop! the thought in its tracks. Every time you allow the thought to blossom fully formed in your head, you increase the chances it will stay there and make you nervous and *feel welcome to come back tomorrow.* You reinforce the connections in your brain that create that thought.

So stop it before it gets formed.

"What if I go to the party and no one talks to me? Stop!

"What if I go to the party and ..." Stop!

"What if I go to ..." Stop!

"Wha..." Stop!

Keep doing this until you Stop! the thought. If you can say Stop! out loud (without people stopping and staring at you), that is best. Otherwise, do it in your head.

Strategy 2: Mindfulness

Mindfulness is a Buddhist concept. It means *staying in the here and now.* Anything that keeps your mind here and now instead of in the future will calm you mentally and physically. This can be physical exercise, playing a game, singing, talking to a friend—anything!

However, you need to experiment. The activities that work for you will differ from those that work for me. Nothing will work unless you discipline yourself to stop thinking about your fear and *do something else.*

The more I work with people who suffer from anxiety, depression, or both, the more convinced I am that they need to learn mindfulness. They need to find a quiet time every day and practice being peaceful. I strongly recommend meditation. If you think you can't meditate, think again. If you know how to worry and ruminate, you know how to meditate.

For those of you with children who have anxiety or attention problems, see *Building Emotional Intelligence* in Further Reading. This book advocates the practice of having a quiet time with your child on a regular basis. The author suggests that this will help your child with anxiety and will help focus their attention.

If you are interested in Mindfulness, you can read more in the book, *Mindfulness in Plain English*, available as a free download on the Internet.

Strategy 3: Reframing

Recognizing that you are scaring yourself and making a joke of it will help. Find a new way to characterize your fear.

Suppose that when you are going to a party, you make dire predictions such as: "What if I go to the party and nobody talks to me?" Is it common for you to have such thoughts before social events? Then you really know it is nonsense, right? So why not have some fun with it.

Reframe it as: "What if I go to that party and everyone comes up to me and won't leave me alone for a minute. They'll be asking so many questions that I'll say, LEAVE ME ALONE AND STOP TALKING TO ME!" That would be new. Reframing involves having some phun with your phobias.

Strategy 4: Targeting your FEAR

This one is not, strictly speaking, cognitive or behavioral. Targeting your fear requires more introspection and self-examination. Anxiety is not a state of being; it is a process you control.

Our fears are tied to how we approach the world. It takes some effort to identify our "anxiety-producing patterns" and replace them with more effective behavior.

To continue our party example: if you do get sweaty palms in social situations, then you need to be willing to look at *how you bring that about.* Notice I didn't say, figure out why you have anxiety in social situations. I said, *How do you make your anxiety happen?*

How do you approach social situations? What do you do before, during, and after a social situation? Do you obsess over what to wear? Do you remind yourself of every embarrassing thing that ever happened to you? Afterward, do you relive the entire party, critiquing every little thing you said and did? What can you do to change these self-defeating behaviors?

Get some input from people who do not appear to share your anxieties. Ask them how they behave in social situations or if they ever feel anxious and what they do about it. Targeting your fears means learning the details of how you create your anxieties.

The goal is to figure out what you are doing to *make yourself fearful, and then change it*. This requires thinking differently about your behavior. You may find you need the help of a good psychotherapist.

Those are the four basic techniques for managing anxiety. None of these solutions will work if you persist in thinking that you have no control over your anxieties. When they do work, they are what we called in the business world, "workarounds." They do not solve the problem. The solution to your anxiety lies in admitting to yourself what you are avoiding or grasping by being anxious.

Good luck and remember what author, Leo Buscalia, once said:

> *"What are we so afraid of? None of us is going to get out of this {life} alive anyway!"*

The Breath of Life

I've often noticed that the people who come to see me don't breathe fully. I barely see their chests move at all. When your breathing is shallow, you make your brain nervous. The brain stem is the oldest part of the brain and its job is to regulate activities: sleep cycle, heart rate, and breathing, to name a few.

When we can't breathe, the brain stem is not happy and it initiates counter-measures to get us breathing again. You can hold your breath for a time, but not long because our brains will not tolerate it. All kinds of alarms go off.

To the brain, it doesn't matter if you can't breathe because there is no air or because you are not breathing effectively. The brain responds by sending chemicals to alert you to the problem. Your heart rate goes up, your stress hormones increase, and your sense of well-being and safety go down. KEEP BREATHING! Here endeth the lesson.

Stop Being Anxious and Start Being Anxious

The *American Heritage College Dictionary* provides the following definitions of the word "anxious": "uneasy and apprehensive about something uncertain; " and "eagerly and earnestly desirous"

It gives the derivation of the word as: "from Latin angere – to torment."

As Mr. Spock would say, "fascinating." How can the same word mean worried, as in, "he was anxious about his date with Penelope," and eager, as in, "the children were anxious for Christmas to come?"

Why do we get anxious-worried about things that we ought to be anxious-excited about? I don't think the answer is hard to figure out. "Excited" sometimes leads to "disappointed."

If you don't get too excited about that date with Penelope or Edgar, you will not feel so disappointed if he or she calls up the day before and cancels because the boss sent him or her to Cleveland on business.

Excitement sometimes leads to disappointment.

How do you *not get excited* about something exciting?

You worry. What if the date doesn't go well? What if it rains all week during my vacation in Hawai'i? What if tomorrow is the last day of the world? *What if, what if, what if*—those two little words are the tool of a lot of self-torment (anxiety). If I can torment myself enough, then I don't have to be disappointed when life hands me a clunker.

What if, instead of saying I'm having an anxiety attack, people said:

"I am having a self-tormenting attack"

Or

"I am worrying in order to avoid the risk of disappointment?"

What if I stopped being anxious-worried and started being anxious-excited?

Believing in Magic

In 1981, Stephen King published *It*, a novel about a monster that terrorizes a small town in Maine. The monster manifests to people in many forms, but the most common is a white faced clown named Pennywise. You may have seen the TV miniseries some years ago.

The main characters are a group of seven children who band together to fight Pennywise in 1958. He returns in 1985, and they're now adults and have to fight again. While the front-story is a horror story, the back-story is about childhood and how children handle fear differently from adults. The kids believe that they, as a group, have a special power and they exercise this power in illogical, childlike ways that often work.

For example, the monster confronts one of the kids when he's alone. Terrified, the child pulls out his "bird catalog," bird watching being his hobby, and begins reciting the names of birds. He holds the catalog in front of him like a cross against a vampire, and it drives the monster away. Since he believes in the catalog and its truth, it becomes his talisman.

A talisman is a magic spell, often called a "ward," meant to repel something bad or keep something bad from happening. "Warding off" is often cited as the basis of worrying. Worrying becomes the ward or talisman to keep something from happening.

As adults, we have more difficulty connecting with our power and believing in it. Our rational minds get in the way. We prefer to believe in disorders and medications rather than our control over our fears. Symbols can help us focus our power. We need to find positive and healthful talismans to believe in. Spiritual beliefs and symbols often fill this function.

Magic only works for children, you may be thinking.

I would ask you to consider this. How do we create our fears? We imagine the bad things that could happen to us, and we make them real in our imagination. Then we tell ourselves they *are real*. Does that sound like casting a magic spell to you? If you can cast a spell to create your fears, you can cast a spell to dispel them.

Bill Cosby once performed a comedy routine about "having your music with you when you are alone at night." You hum your music as you walk down the street and nothing can hurt you. I used to do that. Did you? It worked.

What talismans can you hold out against your fears? What do you have faith in that is more powerful than your anxiety?

Living with Uncertainty

I thought it was the right road to turn on. The sign said M-50 and I vaguely recalled the intersection. I turned left and headed east. Suddenly, I felt that gnawing feeling in my stomach that said "maybe this isn't the right road to get to I-69. Maybe I was wrong."

My GPS would tell me the truth. It would reassure me that I had made the right decision. At the moment, it was not showing a large enough area. I reached down intending to touch the screen and zoom out.

Even a small twinge of anxiety is unpleasant. I am especially nervous about getting lost or not knowing where I am. I can turn uncertainty into full blown anxiety. You know the drill.

If I am on the wrong road, I may miss I-69 altogether. I could go miles out of my way. I would be way behind schedule and not make it back to Chicago in time for my social engagement this afternoon. Then I would feel stupid. This last flourish of self-recrimination brings out the nerves.

What is this about? I am uncertain and uncertainty is uncomfortable. Many people who suffer from anxiety tell me they need to be more self-confident. They think that self-confidence is the lack of uncertainty. They are wrong.

Self-confidence is the willingness to live with uncertainty. Self-confidence does not come from making the right decision. Self-confidence comes from knowing you will be fine even when you make a wrong decision.

Will Rogers put it this way: "Good judgment comes with experience and a lot of that comes from bad judgment."

If I turned onto the wrong road, I will eventually find the interstate. The worst thing that will happen is that I am going to see some new real estate along the way. I have to live with my uncertainty for a few minutes.

I removed my hand away from the GPS, took a deep breath and plunged into the unknown.

The next time you feel uncertain about a decision, trust your instincts. If you discover you were right, you will increase your self-trust. If not, smile and pat yourself on the back for having had the confidence to trust your decision. Most important, live with the uncertainty of not knowing for sure.

What You Can Do With Your To-Do List

Many of us use a To-Do list. It can be a helpful tool to relieve anxiety. Once a thing is on our To-Do list, we can stop worrying about forgetting to do it. There are, however, some pitfalls. A friend jokingly told me how to drive yourself crazy with a To-Do list.

Here is his rather facetious advice:

"Used properly, a To-Do list can provide endless restless nights and days of indigestion. If you're not getting enough anxiety out of your To-Do list, then you aren't doing it right. First, you have to keep that list current with everything you think you have to do. The minimum length for a proper To-Do list is fifty or sixty items. Any fewer than that and you probably are forgetting something. You can't worry about something you have forgotten.

"Assign a numerical code (1 to 10) to each item where "1" is not worth worrying about and "10" is a sleep buster. There may be an iphone app for this. The sum of all your numerical codes is your worry index. This provides an objective measure of how much you should be worrying. The benefit of this is obvious. You now know when you are not worrying enough.

"The worry ratings also tell you the order of priority in getting things done. You could get the ones, twos, and threes done right away. They are not worth worrying about. Put off doing the eights, nines, and tens. They will wake you in a cold sweat night after night.

"The middle numbers are where you have wiggle room. Get enough of these items done to fine tune your level of worry and keep it exactly where you are most comfortable. If you find you're not worrying enough, increase the worry ratings of some of those ones, twos and threes. Maybe you underrated some of them. Post your To-Do list where you can see it all the time. Hang it in multiple places. Put it on your Face Book page and on your cell phone.

"There is no end to the creative ways you can use a To-Do list to remind yourself to worry."

My thanks to my friend, who prefers to remain anonymous, for putting some perspective on To-Do lists.

Speaking of Behavior

We manipulate our world by the words we choose to describe it. One way we do this is by talking about ourselves as a state of being. For example, "I am depressed" or "I am anxious." Another way is using words that avoid responsibility such as "I have to." Both make us powerless. Taking responsibility for who we are and what we're doing or not doing makes us powerful.

One way to change our world is to change the way we talk about it. Here are some examples to get you started.

Powerless words: I am in a bad mood.
Taking Responsibility: I am choosing a bad mood

Powerless words: I am depressed.
Taking Responsibility: I am depressing my emotions to avoid feeling (fill in the blank)

Powerless Words: I am nervous (anxious, scared).
Taking Responsibility: I am scaring myself about (what?) to avoid (what?)

Powerless Words: I can't.
Taking Responsibility: I choose not to or I won't.

Powerless Words: Life is hard.
Taking Responsibility: I sometimes make life hard.

Powerless Words: I have to (go to work).
Taking Responsibility: I choose to (go to work) because the alternative is (poverty)

Powerless Words: I should (shouldn't)
Taking Responsibility: Of the options I have, choice A is better because it will benefit me in the following ways: (list them)

These are a few examples of changing our language to be more in charge of our lives. Notice that the powerless words give control to something other than ourselves while the responsible words take control back inside of us.

Why We Do What We Do.

"I earnestly believe, however, that an important form of self-compassion is to make choices motivated purely by our desire to contribute to life, rather than out of fear, guilt, shame, duty, or obligation" (Marshall Rosenberg, *Nonviolent Communication: A Language of Life*, p. 135.)

We often say things like "I have to go to work," "I have to pay my bills," or "I have to go to my wife's family reunion this weekend."

"Have to, have to, have to" is so common an expression that we hardly even think about it. Do you have to go to work? "Of course I do," you respond. Why do you have to go to work? "Because I need money," you respond. Why do you need money? "To pay my bills," you respond. Why do you want to pay your bills?

About this time, you would be looking at me as if I am an idiot. However, the ultimate answer to these questions is that you choose to go to work, to earn money, to pay your bills, and to pay for all the things you want to do. You make that choice. No one forces you to do any of these things.

"I have a family and kids," you say. "I have to support them. It's my responsibility." Of course it's your responsibility. Why do you have that responsibility? You chose it. You chose to have children. Why did you do that?

If you're being honest, you are feeling sheepish at this point, because your excuses for why you do these things are looking like excuses. You chose to have children, because you wanted the joy of having children. You go to work and support them because you love them.

"Okay," you rejoin, with a stubborn look in your eyes, "I go to work and support my kids because I love them. I'll give you that. But my job sucks."

That may be true. You may not like the job you have now. That goal ought to be at the top of your goal list: "Find a job I really like." Before you do that, you might want to give some thought to why you hate your job. Otherwise, you won't know what you're looking for when you start your job hunt. I want to tell you about a man I knew in the corporate world when I was a computer programmer. We'll call him Ben.

Most of us had complaints about our jobs and the company we worked for and the stupidity of government regulations that we had to comply with. Complaining is a high form of art in most organizations.

Many companies let their employees go home early on Christmas Eve. I once heard a woman complain that this was a dumb policy because some people don't have families to go to and they would be better off staying at work. I imagined she was lonely.

Ben never complained, not that I heard anyway. One day we were sitting at lunch, complaining, and someone mentioned Ben. "What's his thing?" a coworker asked. Sometimes the universe hears a question and delivers an answer. Just then, Ben joined our table.

"Ben, we were talking about you and saying that you never complain about anything. What is your secret? If it's drugs, can you share some with the rest of us?"

Ben laughed. "What's to complain about?" he said. "I have a good job, I make a good salary. And every night I go home to the best wife and kids in the world."

Some uncomfortable smiles erupted at this—and a couple frowns. "But Ben, what about your career here? Do you have any ambition? Last month, someone else got the promotion you should have gotten. How long have you been at your pay grade?"

"Why would I want a promotion? I'd have to spend more hours at work."

"But Ben, you'd make more money, have a better life."

"I don't need more money. My wife and kids are my life."

That was a conversation stopper. What do you say to a man who thinks he has it all? What right does he have to be that happy and content?

Did Ben like his job? Who knows? What Ben had that most people don't is that he knew what was important to him. He knew exactly what he wants from his life at that time. Going to work was play for him because it allowed him to love, support, and care for his family.

When we stop making excuses for why we do what we do and start admitting that we chose these things, we stop feeling sorry for ourselves because we did not get the promotion or the best assignment or we don't like our boss. We either decide to like our life, or we change it in some way to make it better. Complaining is a way of boiling away energy instead of changing our lives.

> *Going to work was play for him because it allowed him to love, support, and care for his family.*

When Rosenberg says, "make choices motivated purely by our desire to contribute to life," I think he means, find the positive reasons we do things and focus on those, rather than believing that we have to do them.

Then you will know what is working in your life and what isn't and that will tell you what you need your goals to be.

Setting Goals When You are Unemployed.

Ten years ago, I was a computer programmer, employed by a financial institution. I had made my living in that field for thirty years. I was in my fifties, bored, out of date, a dinosaur in my field. I had to ask myself: *What do I want to be when I grow up?*

I changed careers, and went into the mental health field. Today, as I watch the unemployment statistics (9.4% in Illinois, as of January, 2012) I'm concerned about the emotional effects of unemployment on individuals. Other than not getting a paycheck, what does it mean to not have a job?

The most obvious thing is that you have too much time. Work structures our time: when you go to bed at night, when you get up, what you will be doing for eight or more hours a day. Less obviously, it tells you when you are free to do other things. Your non-work time is yours. If you don't have a job, when can you relax?

Many of us equate our self-worth with what we do to make money or how much money we make. This reality thundered into my life when I changed careers and my income dropped by two-thirds. When I received my first paycheck at the social service agency where I first worked after graduation, I felt physically ill. I opened the paycheck with my eyes closed.

I was embarrassed to tell friends what I was making. I would never have shown them the place I worked. I was used to working in a corporate environment that was well maintained and equipped. We had state-of-the-art computers, meeting rooms with comfortable chairs, and a company subsidized cafeteria. There were rewards, bonuses, corporate parties with lavish food, business trips.

Now I was working in an office that had not had a coat of paint in this century. My office didn't have a window. The carpeting needed cleaning. My computer came to this country on the Mayflower.

My self-image took a beating. I did not feel valued by my employer. I had made the choice to work there, and I still was affected by the physical and financial realities of my position.

When people are unemployed, it's worse. When we aren't doing something that we identify as valuable, it's hard to feel valuable. We dread that question: "So, George, what do you do?" Any answer other than to say how we earn money seems unacceptable.

Having a job makes us feel as if we are part of the world. We talk about our jobs, even in social settings. Work is part of our shared culture. When we have no work, we can feel like an outsider.

When you don't have a job, it's hard enough not making a paycheck, but what can you do about the emotional consequences? Here are some possible goals when you are unemployed:

- *Look at your time as an opportunity. Identify things you like doing that you didn't have time for before. Start doing them.*
- *Structure your day. Get up at roughly the same time and go to bed at roughly the same time at night.*
- *If you're job hunting, spend part of the day doing that and part of it doing the things you like doing. Set specific job hunting goals: how many resumes you will send each day, how many phone calls.*
- *Find your talents and strengths. These are "who you are," not "what you do."*
- *Find a place to belong. This may be a volunteer gig or a social activity. Get out there and live. Have some fun.*
- *Be open to opportunities. Your old job or career may be gone forever. You may have to reinvent yourself.*

Further Reading

Demasio, Antonio (2000), *The Feeling of What Happens: Body and Emotion in the Making of Consciousness*, Mariner Books
If you want to understand more about how emotions work, this is recommended. Well written and readable, this book explains what we have learned about the brain and emotion in recent years.

LeDoux, Joseph (1998), *The Emotional Brain: The Mysterious Underpinnings of Emotional Life*, Simon & Schuster
This very readable book describes research into the nature of how our brains process emotions.

LeDoux, Joseph (2003), *Synaptic Self: How Our Brains Become Who We Are*, Penguin Books
This book is more technical and harder to read, but if you want to understand how the brain works, this is good place to start.

Venerable H. Gunaratana Mahathera (1990), *Mindfulness in Plain English*,
Available for download as a pdf file, www.urbandharma.org
This is a how to manual for those who wish to learn meditation.

Lantieri, Linda (2008), *Building Emotional Intelligence*, Sounds True
For those of you with kids that have anxiety or attention problems, this books promotes the use of daily quiet time, relaxation, and meditation, done with your child. A CD is included with the hard copy edition that contains guided relaxation exercises.

Berne, Eric (1996), *Games People Play: The Basic Handbook of Transactional Analysis*, Ballantine Books
One of the most readable and insightful books ever written on human behavior.

Rosenberg, Marshall B. (2003), *Non-Violent Communication: A Language of Life,* Puddledancer Press
Violence often begins with words. There are so many reasons to read Rosenberg's book, I could never list them. Here are a few: Learn how to express compassion for yourself and others; learn how to use anger in effective ways; learn how to keep your emotional balance in conflict situations; learn to talk more effectively with your kids.

Peters, Tom (2004), *In Search of Excellence: Lessons from America's Best Run Companies*, Harper Business
Peters set the pattern for much of the thinking in corporate America. His views are still timely.

Schwartz, Jeffrey (1997), *Brainlock: Free Yourself From Obsessive Compulsive Behavior*, Harper Perennial
For those of you that believe your anxieties are due to a brain disorder that you have no control over, Dr. Schwartz's work on OCD will be enlightening.

The American Psychiatric Association (2000), *The Diagnostic and Statistical Manual of Mental Disorders DSM-IV-TR*, Amer Psychiatric Pub
In the United States, this is the bible on mental disorders. Pages 429 to 484 define the ten or so Anxiety Disorders. You probably don't want to buy this, but your local library will have a copy.

www.ingramcontent.com/pod-product-compliance
Lightning Source LLC
Chambersburg PA
CBHW071817020426
42331CB00007B/1520